Media and Monarchy in Sweden

Media and Monarchy in Sweden

Mats Jönsson & Patrik Lundell (eds.)

NORDICOM

Media and Monarchy in Sweden

Mats Jönsson & Patrik Lundell (eds.)

ISBN 978-91-89471-77-1

Published by:
Nordicom
University of Gothenburg
Box 713
SE 405 30 Göteborg
Sweden

Cover by: Daniel Zachrisson
Cover photo: IMS/Nordic Photos
Printed by: Livréna AB, Göteborg, Sweden, 2009
Environmental certification according to ISO 14001

Contents

Acknowledgements

Our gratitude goes to King Gustaf VI Adolf's Fund for Swedish Culture (Stiftelsen Konung Gustaf VI Adolfs fond för svensk kultur) and The Royal Patriotic Society (Kungl. Patriotiska Sällskapet) for their financial contributions to the completion of this book. And thanks Karen Williams, for improving our English, and Nordicom, for publishing it.

Lund, March 2009

Mats Jönsson & Patrik Lundell

Media and Monarchy

An Introduction

Mats Jönsson & Patrik Lundell

Contrary to the media, the monarchy is an institution that rarely alters its manners and appearances, but rather excels in fixed traditions and rituals. Modern monarchy is therefore sometimes seen as an atavism, incommensurable with existing ideas of a democratic and egalitarian political culture.[1] But because monarchies are obviously still thriving – not least in the media – we are probably far less modern than we like to think.[2] This, in turn, suggests that the conservative constancy that royal institutions offer and personify constitutes a major reason for their obvious attraction in our contemporary society. Just to take an example, the largest Swedish publishing house, Bonnier, started a "high quality glossy magazine" baptized *Queen* in the spring of 2008. A key sales argument, besides an alleged growing public demand for royal glamour in general, was an explicit focus on "history".[3] In the editorial of the first issue, it was additionally claimed that the lives of the royals encompass much of "our history" and "our heritage".[4]

We seem to be witnessing a revival and renaissance for royalty in the Swedish media today, and just as elsewhere, the coverage is predominantly directed at a domestic audience. The heterogenic examples of Swedish royal mediations analysed here have more in common with their foreign equivalents than they have characteristics setting them apart. The relations between monarchy and media in Sweden should therefore predominantly be seen as metonymic examples of a European, if not global, tendency within modern celebrity and media culture, whose focus is increasingly directed at the private and intimate aspects of the royals. In this book, nine scholars from six academic disciplines within the humanities and the social sciences put this and other contemporary tendencies in historical perspective. We have done so in the hope of making past, present and future events within media and monarchy in Sweden more understandable, but naturally also because we want to reveal the complex discourses at work within and between these two powerful institutions.

Royal Public Service

When writing this introduction, three separate royal events were launched in the media within a couple days' time. In all three cases, Swedish public service television (SVT) was directly involved. The first incident occurred on 2 June 2008, when SVT transmitted the investigatory and controversial programme "His Royal Highness Westling", in which a new royal trend was put forth.[5] In brief, it was claimed that royal families have become more and more mundane, which in turn has enabled individuals with a common background to wed into formerly almost untouchable social strata. Using the examples of Norway, Denmark, Holland and Spain, the reporters and their interviewees unanimously concluded that Sweden was to follow this trend as soon as Crown Princess Victoria married her fiancé, the workout instructor Daniel Westling. One of the more interesting theses, confirmed by prominent journalists as well as by the Head of The House of Nobility, was that this new development has meant that traditional guardians of the Crown – such as the nobility and the upper class – are becoming increasingly sceptical of royals, and that the working class therefore constitutes the most active and fervent defender of the monarchy today.

The second case of SVT-mediated monarchy was launched on the Swedish national day, 6 June, which in itself encompasses the tension between tradition and modernity; 6 June is the day when Gustavus Vasa was elected king in 1523, but it is also the day when Sweden's modern constitution was signed in 1809. This time the event came in the form of a new blogspot on the Internet exclusively devoted to the Swedish royal family and court, "The Royal House".[6] Among other things, the site provides its user with various SVT productions about the royal family as well as a complete genealogical tree. The third and final royal media event also took place on the national day, when SVT, once again, broadcast live from the festivities at the open-air museum Skansen on Royal Djurgården in Stockholm. On this symbolic national platform *par preference*, the royal Bernadotte family not only attends nationalistic rituals as the most prominent and symbolically important guests of honour, but naturally also functions as a main media attraction in real life, on live TV and soon afterwards in various other media. In fact, the presence of public service television at Skansen arguably played a decisive role when 6 June finally became a Swedish national holiday three years ago.

What these three examples show is that public service television plays a central, if not indispensable, role for the Swedish monarchy today, a role for which SVT has been critisized repeatedly. In our view, a keyword for understanding mainstream royal mediations of this kind is *proximity*, for as Michael Maffesoli concluded, "the image is no longer distant, overarching, totally abstract, but rather it is defined by proximity".[7] The aforementioned magazine *Queen* thus assures us that it, due to its "unique connections", will contain no insidious gossip but instead "inside news", at the same time emphasizing that "a European princess is closely tied to the editorial staff"; we are offered, in other words, exclusive insights into the private quarters of royal life.[8] The editor's welcome to the readers further emphasizes this tendency in that it is launched under the heading "Personal".[9] Indeed, in the two issues of *Queen* that have been published thus far, the personal angle vis-à-vis the Swedish royal family already becomes evident on the covers, where the main headlines take the form of direct addresses to the Swedish princesses: "Victoria, Marry Daniel!" and "Madeleine, Here Is Your Life!", respectively.

The Swedish periodical *Queen* launches seemingly intimate relations to the country's two princesses by addressing them directly on the covers of its first two issues. *Queen*, 2008 (1 and 2).

Moreover, in his recent book on European monarchies, Guido Knopp devotes an entire chapter to the Swedish royal family. Refraining from any distant or general perspective, he deliberately applies a personal and detailed angle on the Bernadotte family, rhetorically describing them as "Persil-Variants of monarchy: attractive, sympathetic and, above all, without scandals".[10]

Based on the above, we argue that today's numerous mediations of royals and court members constitute telling examples of how the media relentlessly try to make well-known, yet distant, figures of prominence more familiar and closer to the common man. And this state of affairs can naturally also be traced in consumers' responses. For instance, during about the same period as our Swedish examples above occurred, the June issue of the British periodical *Royalty Monthly* was published. As would be expected, this magazine puts the British royal family in the centre of attention, but in a final section called "Last Word, The Pages Where Our Readers Have Their Say", the main question of the June issue exclusively dealt with the Swedish throne. The letter was sent in by Mrs E. Christopher from Surrey, England, who wanted to know more about the Swedish Crown Princess Victoria.[11]

Just as the demand put forward by the periodical *Queen*, the prayers of Mrs E. Christopher and like-minded royalists were recently answered when Crown Princess Victoria on February 24 2009 finally said "Yes" to Mr. Daniel Westling. *GT* February 25 2009.

In many ways, Mrs Christopher constitutes what one might call a typical royalist of today, characterized by an affective and personal relation to monarchies in general and to one specific royal person in particular. More to the point, Mrs Christopher specifically asks for increased visual exposure of Victoria in order to preserve and cherish this close yet mediated bond even more. Her affectively driven interest in royalties becomes most apparent in the ways in which she seeks to strengthen her imaginary connection to the Swedish crown princess using rhetorical formulations and hypothetical assumptions, which, incidentally, all are based on information taken from the media. Consequently, this is a representative example of how an individual subject in the private sphere tries to become intimate with and delve into the personal affairs of a famous celebrity in the public sphere.

New as these phenomena may seem, and in some aspects surely are, important yet quasi-intimate relations between the common man and royalties have existed and flourished for centuries. A class-related shift in royal defenders, for example, might be true in a shorter historical perspective and thus partly explain the present increasing demand for monarchy in the popular media in Sweden. If the historical horizon is widened, however, the picture becomes far more complicated. Even if an explicit media focus has been absent, historical studies into these relations have long testified to this. Recent research, including works such as *Media, Monarchy, and Power* (2003) and *Majestät!* (2006) to name but two, has addressed these questions in more thorough and partly new ways. Confirmed here is the fact that the complex interrelations between media and monarchy in part *have* changed over the centuries, not least owing to radical shifts in the technology's ability to get closer to the royal objects of interest. But at the same time, many aspects of the mutual media-monarchic usage have remained more or less the same.[12] A striking definition of this paradoxical mix of an almost unaltered royal base and a constantly shifting medial superstructure was formulated in Holland in 2001, when the Dutch royal family was described as "Big Brother with a family tree."[13]

Generally, Swedish royals are no exceptions to this constant, yet dynamic, development at work within both media and monarchy. Therefore, the examples put forth here should primarily be seen as representative of how most European courts over the years have acted and positioned themselves on the public arena. The reason we say *most* European courts is that the British monarchy stands out as an exception. For instance, Neil Blain and Hugh O'Donell have shown that it has rarely been "required to justify itself by its contribution to political modernity" in the same way as the other courts in Europe have.[14] Still, the exclusive focus on analysing and historicizing the Swedish monarchy is justified by the fact that royal public appearances are fairly similar everywhere, notwithstanding national differences in their specific expressions. Accordingly, our national perspective reveals how complex encounters between the media and monarchy have functioned throughout the years in Sweden, on the one hand, while it puts particularly Swedish issues in relation to general media-monarchic tendencies in other countries, on the other.

Not only do we believe that analyses of older media strategies vis-à-vis monarchy shed light on contemporary equivalents domestically and abroad, we also think that studies into present-day conditions offer new ways of looking at older types of royal mediations. We are convinced, for instance, that the ways in which the monarchy navigates in a new digital media landscape can be better understood through insights into older media strategies; just as the present conditions open our eyes to monarchic relations to "new media" in the past. And, in fact, the same can be said about open attitudes towards the concept of media in general. Thus in this book, and based on the belief that these approaches can be mutually enriching, media forms such as altars and statues are taken just as seriously as traditional mass media. This point of departure opens up for a broad spectrum of studies into the interrelations between media and monarchy, ranging from media-informed investigations into the phenomenon of monarchy to monarchy-oriented media studies.

Diachronic Monarchy

History never comes to us unmediated. Most people's images of the Swedish eighteenth century king Gustavus III, to briefly discuss a tangible example, have above all been shaped by various forms of present-day media products on history in the form of books, articles, novels, films, TV programmes, theatre plays, and exhibitions. In other words, these images are fashioned by today's predominating forms of historiography.

Our conception of how monarchs have looked in the past is constantly confirmed or challenged by the media. Here in the form of a drama about King Gustavus III that was broadcast on Swedish public service television in 2001. *Photo:* SVT Archive, 2001.

However, not even to the historian does history come unmediated. The historian, of course, does not simply transform empirical facts into historical knowledge. The past can *only* be reached with the help of various mediated statements. A historical figure such as Gustavus III can thus be studied through his letters and recorded speeches, through the medallions he had struck and the impressive buildings he had commissioned, as well as through the orders he sent out and the ordinances he promulgated. Our understanding of him can be further enriched by traces in various archival materials (other persons' letters and diaries, for example), by newspapers (official reports, obsequious appraisals or disguised criticism), and by a spectrum of artistic products (handwritten poems, printed novels, pencil-drawings, oil paintings, bronze statues). Put together, all these artefacts and documents constitute an ever-expanding media archive offering limitless perspectives on this particular monarch.

Moreover, we could take an interest in Gustavus III as a media producer, naturally not forgetting that he was an important patron of the arts and of literature. Another approach would be to study him as media content, as well as ask what kind of media he consumed and to what effect. Perhaps we could even analyse him *as* a medium – how he, in person or further mediated, carried certain symbolic meanings. Of course, trying to understand how all these roles were entangled constitutes yet another strategy. In addition, we could choose to analyse Gustavus III's influence on the cultural, political and legal conditions of the production, distribution and consumption of media during his reign. When trying to answer questions related to these various lines of inquiry, we obviously cannot approach the media archive as a simple and transparent container of "facts". The eighteenth century terms of media production, the media laws and conventions, including those concerning archival conditions, as well as genre systems, conceptual shifts and historically changed ways of seeing and reading different media forms, all constitute fundamental factors that are imperative if we wish to properly understand this specific king and his impact.

Additionally, most of our contemporary experiences are naturally also imbedded in an ever-expanding range of media output. Few of us have, for instance, any direct access to the present Swedish king, Carl XVI Gustaf. Instead, we "meet" him in the tabloids, in royal yearbooks, on the Internet, on chocolate boxes, on postcards, on our coins, and on TV. Should we actually see him in person, it would most likely be in the context of a more or less official and symbolic act, waving from a balcony, receiving flowers from a child, giving a speech. And if we bumped into him during an incognito holiday trip and exchanged a few words with him, would that really be His Majesty the King or just the person who otherwise plays a part in an ongoing official drama? Royal proximity is thus primarily an illusion that is being kept alive and taken advantage of by the media – as well as by the monarchy itself. In other words, we never really get to see the Emperor's new clothes; we only learn about them or their absence via various forms of media.

Consequently, royals are sometimes mere objects of media interest, sometimes (within given limitations) they are in charge of the content, and sometimes they even play the roles of media themselves. But most importantly, whatever part they take or are given, their performances are always intertwined with media in complex ways. This is of course not unique to analyses of monarchy, as information – historical or contemporary – is always formed by prevailing media conditions. As Robert Darnton concluded: "Every age was an age of information, each in its own way."[15] The technological, social, cultural and economical features of the media at any given time (and of the media archive over time) thus have a profound influence on what can be said and done and what is actually accessible, both in real time and in a historical perspective. In this sense, the study of media and monarchy is of course unlimited.

Media perspectives on monarchs or monarchies, however, can also be of a more fundamental character. We can look at these agents and institutions as primarily media phenomena or media constructions. From this perspective, their functions and meanings cannot be separated from media issues. For instance, in *Queen Victoria: First Media Monarch* (2003), John Plunkett convincingly argues that the rise of modern mass media reinvented the position of the monarchy in national life, a perspective echoing Eric Hobsbawm and Terence Ranger's seminal anthology *The Invention of Tradition* (1983).[16] Furthermore, in his contribution to the latter book, David Cannadine discusses one of the most influential British politicians during the reign of Victoria, William Gladstone, who repeatedly "reminded the queen of the 'vast importance' of the 'social and visible functions of the monarchy'".[17] Indeed, when criticizing Queen Victoria for having retired from almost all official duties during the 1870s, the economist – and journalist – Walter Bagehot even went so far as to conclude that: "to be invisible is to be forgotten", adding that "to be a symbol, and an effective symbol, you must be vividly and often seen."[18] Thus, seeing royal symbols and believing in the actual monarchy have largely been dependent on each other, and the deciding factor has been whether or not the royal individual in question is sufficiently exposed and presented in the public sphere. Undoubtedly, Mrs Christopher's above-mentioned letter to *Royalty Monthly* emphatically confirms that this need for a constant visual display of royals in the media remains today. In other words, it is doubtful whether a modern unmediated monarchy is at all conceivable.

Certainly, many of our modern notions of monarchy were invented in the nineteenth century. Queen Victoria and her contemporary monarchs in Sweden acted and were acted upon in media landscapes quite differently from only a few decades earlier. However, kings and queens had long before invented traditions and staged themselves, at the same time as they had been staged by other actors. True, Queen Victoria might very well have been the first British modern mass-media monarch (depending on how we define modern mass media), but not even *le Roi Soleil*, as presented in Peter Burke's pioneering work *The Fabrication of Louis XIV* (1992), was the first media-made monarch. Having castles built and parks laid out, having portraits painted, being honoured with poems or ordering chronicles were not new phenomena in the latter half of the seventeenth century.[19]

About the Book

That the majority of the contributions here deal with the Bernadotte family and its reign in Sweden since 1814 must not be understood as a statement in itself.[20] Undoubtedly, these almost two hundred years encompass a very formative period, but the same can be said about, for instance, the print revolution and the consolidation of nation-states in the sixteenth century. And of course, historical continuity is also worth addressing. This book is therefore more a result of the previous research activities of the contributors than it is guided by any kind of teleological perspective on either media or monarchy. That five of the authors jointly held an international conference panel about media and monarchy in 2007 naturally also plays a part in this context.[21] Additionally, the contributions are not gathered around one overall method, theory or model. Instead, we have all been guided by the ambition to present a broad spectrum of ideas on media-monarchic relations in Sweden. As a consequence, the resulting academic smorgasbord is presented in the form of a loose chronology, which not only reveals heterogenic features in the media's depiction of monarchy, but also presents equally complex views on royal usage of media.

In her text, historian *Louise Berglund* shows how Queen Philippa of Sweden, during the early fifteenth century, transformed the altar in the Vadstena Abbey Church into an effective media platform. On the one hand, Berglund's example reveals that medieval royals possessed significant knowledge about the media and their function, while it, on the other hand, shows how difficult it was for a female monarch to reach beyond the enclosed domestic context within which she was more or less entrapped. In his contribution, historian of ideas *Magnus Rodell* casts an eye on the ways in which public monuments of historical royals have been used as mediated means of municipal and national power during the nineteenth century. In the forefront of his discussions are two specific examples, both revealing a number of intricate strategies behind the erection of statues depicting well-known and mythologized Swedish monarchs as well as the actual inaugurations of such monuments.

That royals still can be conceived of, in some sense, as the epitome of celebrity culture is also analysed in media and communication scholar *Kristina Widestedt's* contribution to the book, but she does so from another perspective. In essence, Widestedt examines three Swedish royal weddings in 1888, 1932, and 1976. Hereby, she manages to historically test the relevance and alterations of "the myth of the mediated centre". In particular, she argues for the relevance of using historical sources and developments when trying to understand contemporary media-monarchic relations. Historian of ideas *Patrik Lundell* touches upon this myth from a slightly different angle when challenging a popular genre of historical media studies in which monarchs usually play the evil adversary to the assaulting and liberating newspaper press. Contrary to such an apologetic approach, Lundell studies the fact that the monarchy, both actively and as a symbol, has contributed to the legitimacy of the fourth estate. In particular, he discusses mutual interests and converging strategies that united the monarch and the press in the international press conference in Stockholm in 1897.

Thereafter, historian and film scholar *Tommy Gustafsson* analyses the role of gender when King Charles XII was portrayed as a symbol of hegemonic masculinity in the fiction film *Karl XII* (1925). In his analysis of how this depiction of a legendary monarch has discursively legitimized a specific form of masculinity in Sweden for almost six decades, Gustafsson demonstrates that postponed or delayed history-making can have significant effects on contemporary views on gender. Film scholar *Mats Jönsson's* contribution is partly guided by similar perspectives, but here, the use and presence of the Bernadotte family in the media during World War Two are in the forefront of the investigation. More specifically, Jönsson looks at the ways in which members of the royal family both actively and symbolically participated in a massive national campaign for Swedish military defence in 1940. The Swedish monarchy's relations to and impact on nationalism also constitute the object under study in political scientist *Cecilia Åse's* subsequent chapter. By specifically looking at representations of the female body, gender and sexuality in royal yearbooks and anniversary publications from the past decades, Åse shows that all her examples can be

17

described as expressions of a kind of national pleasure that officially, yet subtly, manifests the continuation of a hetero-normative Swedish realm.

Ethnologist *Mattias Frihammar* presents an even more contemporary analysis, focusing on the ways in which the Swedish monarchy has been presented in the mass media of the twenty-first century. Irony is pinpointed as one of the new and spectacular media strategies for trying to get closer to royal celebrities such as King Carl XVI Gustaf. As Frihammar shows, mundane objects that are ironically used and fragmented in mediated mainstream humour can at the same time strengthen the monarchy's position vis-à-vis postmodern media. Indeed, sometimes these objects can even turn into historical artefacts, which might lead them all the way into the renowned archives of the Royal Armoury, here seen as a form of cultural heritage. In his concluding text, media historian *Pelle Snickars* pinpoints a number of historical contrasts, and he specifically focuses on remarks concerning contemporary multimediations of royalty. The monarchy's increasing lack of control over digital media content is at the centre of the discussions, but Snickars also addresses technological developments during the past decade that have provided people interested in the Swedish royal family with new avenues into the private domains of the monarchy.

Undoubtedly, then, fairly marginal niche media on the Internet will have an impact of significant proportions in the years to come. This impact will be both on the ways in which citizens in the Swedish realm use digital technology to approach the royal family and on how the monarchy presents itself multimedially. That the medially pragmatic Bernadotte dynasty is now in the hands of anonymous media producers on the Internet, for example, can be seen as a significant reason for their, hitherto, almost absent activity in the digital domain. Our book puts such royal mediations into historical perspective, and it does so because we are convinced that a better understanding of present and future media-monarchic relations must always be guided by analyses of similar links in the past.

Notes

1. On the other hand, the Swedish monarchy can, and has been, defined as a democracy because the people want it to remain on the throne. Swedish historian Dick Harrison has, for instance, concluded that: "The monarchy in Sweden remains intact because people want it to be, and from that perspective one could argue that the Swedish monarchy is a democracy". Harrison quoted in Guido Knopp, *Majestät! Die letzten großen Monarchien* (München: Bertelsmann, 2006), p. 23.

2. That modern Western society is less modern than we perhaps like to believe is a central message in Eric Hobsbawm & Terence Ranger (eds), *The Invention of Tradition* (Cambridge: Cambridge University Press, 1983). Compare Louise Phillips, "Media Discourse and the Danish Monarchy: Reconciling Egalitarianism and Royalism", *Media, Culture & Society* 1999 (2), for a discussion of a postmodern, ironic relation to the monarchy.

3. Quoted on the magazine's homepage: http://www.bonniertidskrifter.se/tidningar/queen/ (19 August 2008). For some reason, the title of this Swedish periodical is in English. In this book, and depending on the context, Swedish titles (of films, Websites etc.) are translated either in the text or in the notes. If not stated otherwise, all translations have been done by the

respective author(s). Swedish royals with established names in English or Latin are presented thus, except for the present King Carl XVI Gustaf.

4. Roger Lundgren, "Välkommen till Queen", *Queen* 2008 (1), p. 9.
5. "Ers kungliga höghet Westling", SVT, 2 June 2008.
6. "Kungahuset", http://www.sveriges-television.com/svt/jsp/Crosslink.jsp?d=92306&a=116586 4&lid=puff_1165864&lpos=rubrik (6 October 2008).
7. Michael Maffesoli, *The Time of the Tribes* (London: Sage, 1996), quoted in Neil Blain & Hugh O'Donell, *Media, Monarchy, and Power* (Bristol: Intellect, 2003), p. 41.
8. http://www.bonniertidskrifter.se/tidningar/queen/ (19 August 2008).
9. See, for example, *Queen* 2008 (1 and 2), p. 9.
10. Knopp, p. 9.
11. Mrs E. Christopher, "Will Sweden's Crown Princess be settling down soon?", *Royalty Monthly* 2008 (11), p. 80.
12. Blain & O'Donell, and Knopp. See also for instance John Plunkett, *Queen Victoria: First Media Monarch* (Oxford: Oxford University Press, 2003) as well as a number of works partly dealing with these questions such as Daniel Dayan & Elihu Katz, *Media Events: The Live Broadcasting of History* (Cambridge, Mass.: Harvard University Press, 1992) and Margaret Homans & Adrienne Munich (eds), *Remaking Queen Victoria* (Cambridge: Cambridge University Press, 1997).
13. Quote taken from Blain & O'Donnell, p. 11, but originally published in *NRC Handelsblad*, 16 May 2001.
14. Blain & O'Donnell, p. 179.
15. Robert Darnton, "An Early Information Society: News and Media in Eighteenth-Century Paris", *American Historical Review* 2000 (1).
16. Plunkett.
17. David Cannadine, "The Context, Performance and Meaning of Ritual: The British Monarchy and 'The Invention of Tradition', c. 1820-1977", in Hobsbawm & Ranger, p. 119.
18. Ibid.
19. Peter Burke, *The Fabrication of Louis XIV* (New Haven: Yale University Press, 1992).
20. Indeed, the strategies behind and results of the launching of the Bernadottes in Sweden have been analysed in an extensive research project. See, for instance, Mikael Alm & Britt-Inger Johansson (eds), *Scripts of Kingship: Essays on Bernadotte and Dynastic Formation in an Age of Revolution* (Uppsala: Department of History, 2008).
21. The panel, chaired by Mats Jönsson, was called "Media and Monarchy". It was held at INTER: A European Cultural Studies Conference in Sweden, University of Linköping, Campus Norrköping, 11-13 June 2007, and the other participants were Cecilia Åse, Mattias Frihammar, Patrik Lundell, and Kristina Widestedt.

Queen Philippa and Vadstena Abbey

Royal Communication on a Medieval Media Platform

Louise Berglund

In the year 1406, Princess Philippa was married to Eric of Pomerania, king of Denmark, Sweden and Norway. The ceremony took place in Lund Cathedral in Denmark, in what is today the southern part of Sweden. It constituted a prominent public event for the archbishopry and the wedded couple, and it attracted international interest both on a symbolic and a political level. Philippa was the daughter of the English King Henry IV of the Lancastrian house, and her brother was none other than the future King Henry V, one of the most famous medieval English kings. In 1415, King Henry V was to win one of the most illustrious victories in English history when he beat the French at the battle of Agincourt, but he naturally also played a crucial role in the life and actions of his sister. The marriage between Eric and Philippa united two dynasties with great ambitions and precarious holds on power, and it served to strengthen them both. Strengthening and legitimizing positions of power had always been of vital importance to medieval monarchs, especially to someone like Henry IV, who was rumoured to have had his predecessor murdered.[1] But Eric of Pomerania had also come to power in a rather precarious fashion. In 1397, the councils of the three Scandinavian kingdoms had agreed to accept him as their joint king, in order to put an end to the wars and strife that had raged for decades between different candidates for the thrones. The real power figure was not Eric but Queen Margareta, who had adopted him when her own son died. Eric was the son of Margareta's niece.

There were many ways to strengthen and legitimize power. Strategic marriage was one very important instrument, as bids for power were most effective when based on claims of hereditary rights. Another instrument was the major symbolic resource of the Middle Ages, the Catholic Church, with its prelates, monasteries and saints. The states of the Middle Ages were essentially theocracies, in which the limits between secular and religious power were blurred. Kings, queens and other power figures needed the Church, and the Church, in its turn, needed the secular powers. In the medieval political imagination, both institutions wielded different but mutually dependent swords: the worldly sword of kings and aristocrats and the spiritual sword of the men and women of the Church.[2]

As a woman, Philippa was not immediately responsible for either sword. Her marriage to the Scandinavian King Eric had not been arranged by herself but by her father, and was thus not really in her hands. She was eight years old when the marriage was first discussed and twelve when it was formalized. In this strongly patriarchal society, even queens had limited access to instruments of power. Yet one instrument was particularly well suited to them, and that was the one offered by the realm of religion. This was an area in which women as well as men could act openly on the political stage. And for Philippa, it became the media platform *par preference*.

The most prestigious religious institution in fifteenth century Scandinavia was the Birgittine abbey in Vadstena (in Östergötland). Its founder, Saint Birgitta of Sweden, was an internationally recognized, albeit contested, authority on religious and political matters, and the abbey had quickly become the main focus of spiritual life in Scandinavia.[3] It had also emerged as a driving force in the field of political ideology.[4] Birgitta had lived shortly before the events that are to be analysed here, from 1303 to 1373, and had been canonized in 1391. Saint Birgitta and her monastery were the pride of Scandinavia, and the latter thus constituted an important centre for all aspects of cultural, religious and political life until the Reformation. The relationship between Queen Philippa and Vadstena Abbey is the subject of the present discussion. I will argue that during about a decade, in the 1420s, Vadstena Abbey functioned as a media platform for the queen, and in the process I will also discuss the various forms of media available to a public and privileged person of the Middle Ages, a person such as Philippa.

Media in the Middle Ages

Using the concept of media is not self-evident when referring to communication in pre-modern society. In their analysis of media history from the Renaissance to the present, Peter Burke and Asa Briggs note that the term "the media" in its modern sense first appeared in the 1920s.[5] In conjunction with its modern usage, Briggs and Burke employ the term to denote "the communication of information and ideas in words and images".[6] Different forms of communication suit different societies, and usages vary on the basis of many factors. The emergence of the newspaper in the eighteenth century, for instance, was linked to an increase in literacy, socioeconomic changes and technological development. The Middle Ages, on the other hand, was characterized by very low levels of literacy, even among the elite. Other forms of visual communication were therefore imperative to getting the message across, which is part of the reason why it was expressed in many different fashions. One form was art and architecture, another relied on expensive objects such as crowns and jewels, and yet another involved ritualistic performances, especially because "[r]itual, with its strong visual component, was a major form of publicity, as it would be once more in the age of televised events such as the coronation of Queen Elizabeth II".[7]

This is not to say that the written word was not without importance. Books and letters were essential, as they recorded memories and transmitted information. Sermons were an important medium for the transmission of tradition, knowledge, instruction and religious culture, and a vast treasure of written sermons survives from the Middle Ages.[8] In their overview, Briggs and Burke argue that the written word was only gradually accepted as authoritative during the Middle Ages and that people trusted the spoken word above a written document, even if the document had been issued by the Pope. They claim that the rise of written culture occurred as late as the twelfth and thirteenth centuries.[9] There is, however, considerable evidence of the high value placed on writing and books ever since Antiquity, both for practical and for cultural reasons. The Christian religion in itself relies to a great extent on the existence of a sacred Book, and the Church produced a host of other highly valued volumes over the years, containing prayers, hagiographies and other such texts. (This is a tradition that stems from the Jewish roots of Christianity, with the high value placed on the Torah and the works devoted to the Torah and related scriptures.)

In a more prosaic vein, documents were produced to prove that financial and legal arrangements had taken place, and these documents were also very valuable because, hundreds of years afterwards, they could verify ownership and similar matters. In the Middle Ages, however, there was no firm line separating written from visual communication. Holy books were visual objects that were revered by the congregations, and official documents were visual proof of an agreement that had taken place.[10] In medieval Swedish letters, the opening phrase was often something like: "All who hear or see this letter, I greet with God...". In sum, the Middle Ages presented a variety of media, visual and written, that were enduring in the form of objects or texts or more fleeting in the form of rituals or the spoken word. Accordingly, a religious institution such as Vadstena Abbey provided both the means and the setting for employing such discursive practices, not least for a prominent queen such as Philippa.

The Final Resting Place as Media

The most tangible evidence of Philippa's connection with Vadstena Abbey still remains in the Abbey Church. Near the middle of the church, there is a gravestone marking the place where the queen was buried in 1430.[11] Today, the site is simple and unadorned, but this was not the case in the fifteenth century. The grave was placed before an altar, which was subsequently lost during the period after the Reformation. The altar was dedicated to Saint Anne, the mother of the Virgin Mary, and Queen Philippa had financed it. In this way, she had not only chosen the place where she would eventually be buried, but also adorned it in such a way that her generosity and ties to the monastery were visible to all who visited Vadstena Abbey Church – and in the fifteenth century, large numbers of people, living in Sweden and its neighbouring kingdoms or travelling in the area, did. Research into archaeological remains and collections of miracles, for example, show that Vadstena Abbey came to be the most frequently visited holy place in the Nordic countries during the fifteenth century.[12]

The altar was inaugurated in December 1425. The event is recorded in the memorial book of Vadstena Abbey, *Diarium Vadstenense*.[13] According to the entry, the archbishop of Uppsala conducted the ceremony in the presence of the queen, who had specifically requested this. The entry is short and does not provide any further information. The significance of the altar has to be appreciated by combining several other pieces of information. In a later entry, written when the queen was dead, the link between the altar and the grave was made clear in more explicit terms:

> In the Year of our Lord 1430. During the night before twelfth night our beloved queen mistress Philippa died, the queen of Sweden, Denmark and Norway. She was buried here in Vadstena in the choir of Saint Anne, which she herself had founded and had built. She was the very faithful patroness of this monastery and of the whole order.[14]

The foundation is called a choir or a chapel in the many entries, but it seems that it was in fact an altar.[15] Its importance as a medium for the queen can be deduced from a third entry, made in 1459, where it was called "The Queen's Chapel".[16] In fact, it has been remembered as and is still called the Queen's Chapel.

This altar immediately became associated with high symbolic status. A few years after its foundation, it was chosen as the site of the installation of the bishop of Stavanger in Norway by three Swedish bishops.[17] The day of the installation, 18 May, is further significant as it was the feast day of Saint Erik, a twelfth century Swedish king who was hailed as a saint and who, during the course of the late Middle Ages, gradually became one of the most important saints in Sweden, symbolizing good governance and good kingship. In fact, this was why Philippa's husband had been given that name. He was born Count Bogislav in Pomerania, but received the name Eric when Queen Margareta adopted him. The ritual of installing the new bishop of Stavanger might therefore also be seen as a conscious act of highlighting the importance of the king and queen of the three Scandinavian kingdoms.

We do not know how the altar and the grave were adorned, but large funds were donated for that purpose. Among other things, the monastery received two luxurious gold crowns that were to be used either for adorning the altar with two paintings of the coronation of the Virgin Mary or in the coronation ceremonies of future kings and queens. Either way, the importance of Philippa and Eric would be perpetuated, but the subsequent king of the three kingdoms, Karl Knutsson Bonde, did not appreciate this. He had been involved in the final deposition of Eric in 1439 and became king in 1448. In 1454, he came to Vadstena Abbey and demanded that the brothers show him the crowns and other objects donated by Philippa. He then stated that owning such expensive

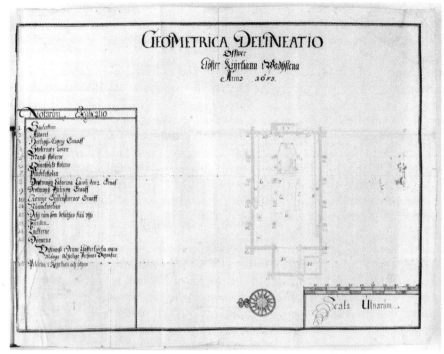

Map of the grave stones in Vadstena Abbey church, from an engraving made in 1653. Gravestone number nine is that of Queen Philippa. The heading reads: Geometrica Delineatio Öffwer Closter Kyrkiann i Wadhstena Anno 1653. Reprint of a geometric drawing from 1653 of the Abbey Church in Vadstena. *Photo:* Uppsala University Library.

objects endangered the souls of the brothers, and took the crowns and other objects with him. Later, the crowns were pawned in Lübeck. Apart from this demonstrating that the symbolic power of such gifts was fully appreciated by others, it is interesting to note that the memorial book entry recording the visit states that the valuables had been donated by Philippa, making no mention of King Eric in that context.[18]

It would appear that the monastery never commissioned the paintings of the coronation of the Virgin for the altar, as the crowns were still there in 1459. This means they had not been sold to finance extensive artwork, and there is no remnant or mention of any such paintings in Vadstena Abbey Church. There is, however, evidence of at least one major work of art provided for the church by Queen Philippa. Among the few remains of the medieval church's ornamentation, which was in all likelihood very rich, there is a wooden sculpture of unusual quality and beauty depicting Saint Anne, holding on her lap the Virgin Mary, who in turn is holding the infant Jesus. Art historians consider it the most valuable decoration in the church from an aesthetic point of view, and there is strong evidence suggesting that Philippa ordered it from the Lübeck artist who created it in 1425, when the altar was inaugurated.[19]

The grave and the altar are placed closer to the entrance of the church than to the front altar. This location appears to have been significant. In a medieval church, the interior is divided into different parts with different purposes, some accessible to the congregation and some closed to them. The front of the church, the chancel, was oriented towards the east, and only accessed by male priests and monks. The largest part of the church, the nave, was for the congregation. In the southern part of Vadstena Abbey, the sisters of the order attended church on an elevated balcony, screened from the congregation. The sepulchre of Philippa is positioned in the nave, close to the centre but on the northern side. This meant that her altar and resting place were situated where the congregation would see them well, and in plain view of the sisters who were on the opposite side. The brothers would have had access to the altar as well.

The altar appears to have been founded in steps. According to a letter dated 25 March 1425, Philippa was in Vadstena and issued a letter founding a cross in the church, a cross devoted to Saint Anne. Her letter states that the abbess and the confessor general were to appoint the chaplain.[20] Philippa had apparently donated funds to finance a chaplain for her altar, an arrangement called prebend (Lat. *prebenda*). Later on, however, in December 1427, she wrote another letter, in which she asked the bishop of Linköping – the diocese in which Vadstena was located – to appoint her own chaplain Petrus Kraka to the prebend of Saint Anne in Vadstena.[21] Some months later, the bishop issued a letter confirming that he was going to do so, apparently being in Vadstena Abbey at the time.[22]

The arrangement surrounding the choir of Saint Anne is mentioned only a few times, but the significance is considerable. It combined the aspect of visual representation in the form of an altar, possibly also a cross, and, eventually, a tombstone, with ritual performances in the form of a chaplain who would be responsible for continuously holding Mass for the Queen and her family members. It is very probable that Philippa had intended for her husband, King Eric, to rest there too. But Eric was ousted from the thrones of the three Scandinavian kingdoms as a result of uprisings in the 1430s, so this never occurred. However, it is fair to say that the work done by Philippa to immortalize her name turned out to be a successful media strategy that both legitimized and manifested the position of her family in the turbulent power struggles of the time.

The Saint is the Message

As mentioned, Philippa had her altar dedicated to Saint Anne and therefore wanted images of the coronation of the Virgin to adorn it. But why did she choose these two saints? If she had been a man, it is probable that she would have preferred to link her foundations to masculine saints such as Saint George, who became an immensely popular figure representing victorious kings and knights in the late Middle Ages, or a royal saint such as Saint Erik of Sweden. In her case, the choice of the two female saints is equally significant.

The cult of the Virgin was of course very important throughout the Middle Ages. The beautiful gold mosaics of the Virgin in Italian churches, such as Santa Maria Maggiore in Rome, testify to the splendour of her cult. The theological aspects of her own conception and that of the Christ were debated, however. Leading theologians were unsure as to the nature of the Virgin's own origins. During the fifteenth century, it was established that Mary herself had been immaculately conceived. Her parents Joachim and Anne had thus not tainted her with mortal sin. In 1481, a feast day celebrating the immaculate conception of Mary was introduced. This establishment of the virginity of Anne was somewhat problematic, however, as it is not supported by any such claims in the Bible.

Saint Birgitta, the founder of Vadstena Abbey, had had many revelations regarding very physical aspects of the birth of Christ and other such events. Her vision of the birth of Christ and the placing of the infant in a cradle became normative for the Church. She also discussed the conception of Mary at length, and concluded that her conception was without sin, because Mary's parents were exceptionally pure people who had an exceptionally chaste marriage. It seems that the revelations of Saint Birgitta helped launch the cult of the mother of Mary in Sweden, and this may explain why Queen Philippa chose to associate herself with that particular saint.[23] The Virgin Mary, on the other hand, was the strong symbol of a heavenly queen, perceived as reigning in splendour with a crown on her head. Therefore, the mediated image of the crowning of Mary did not just underline the importance of queenship and blur the boundaries between the worldly queen and the heavenly one, it also strengthened the gender aspects of medieval royal power with the help of one of the most canonized icons.

However, there may actually be yet another reason for the choice of Saint Anne and the Virgin Mary. Both were also strong symbols of motherhood and the Holy Family. Saint Birgitta may thus have wished to emphasize the importance of Anne because she, like Birgitta, was a holy woman who was not technically a virgin. The persona of Anne demonstrated that even people who had lived in a sexual relationship could be pure, if their marriage had been chaste and primarily oriented towards religion. On the other hand, Philippa may have needed to associate herself with these symbols of family and femaleness for a diametrically opposed reason: She never had any children. When the altar, and probably the sculpture of Saint Anne with Mary and the infant Jesus as well, was commissioned, Philippa had been married for nearly twenty years and had not conceived. When she died five years later, she was still childless. This was of course a problem for her, because she had failed to secure the dynasty of her husband. Although they were parents, both Anne and Mary had been constructed as symbols of virginity, and it is possible that Philippa wished to associate herself with these symbols of purity and spirituality, particularly because, in the Middle Ages, virginity had strong positive connotations of being chosen, special and different from ordinary people. Furthermore, researchers have shown that in later medieval England in particular, "performance of virginity seems to have been an intrinsic part of the enactment of royalty".[24]

27

Many kings, from Edward the Confessor to Richard II, had been constructed as virgin kings, even though they were married. Their childlessness was thus explained as being the result of their devotion to the sacred rather than as stemming from any physical defect.

Gifts and Masses as Media and Memory

Philippa gave generously to Vadstena Abbey while she was alive, and she also remembered it in her will. In doing so, she participated in an important medieval ritual practiced by all Christians. Donating to churches and monasteries was a significant way of inscribing oneself into the community of the religious orders, the parishes and even the realm itself. The records of Vadstena Abbey show that gifts were received even from the relatively poor, although of course the larger gifts from royalty and the elite were commemorated much more explicitly. Nevertheless, as historian Eamon Duffy has highlighted, anyone who donated to a religious institution would be inscribed in the bede-roll, or prayer roll, for all eternity.[25]

Gifts and memory were not, however, a uniform experience. Royalty, naturally, had the resources to invest more heavily than others and they used the status of select monasteries as a way to enhance their own standing. For instance, in England, royalty wished to be buried in Westminster Abbey and remembered there. In Sweden, on the other hand, a succession of monasteries had functioned as royal pantheons. Varnhem Abbey (in Västergötland) had such a function in the twelfth and thirteenth centuries, while the Blackfriars Abbey in Stockholm (now Riddarholmskyrkan) was the main locus in the late thirteenth century. But from the middle of the fourteenth century, the seat of the Birgittine order in Sweden became an attractive burial site for royalty. As early as 1346, long before the monastery was actually built and the order confirmed, King Magnus and Queen Blanche of Namur donated huge sums to the future institution and clearly intended to be buried there.[26] This, however, did not come about.

The donations of Philippa represent a similar tactic, and her personal attentions towards the abbey began in 1415. According to the memorial book, she visited the monastery for a second time that year and apparently stayed for a few days. (There is no record of her first visit.) The brothers showed her the relics of the abbey, and on the following day she asked to be accepted as a sister *ab extra* in the order, a request that was immediately granted. Her mother-in-law, Margareta, had also been a sister *ab extra*, an honour linking the queens to the monastery without affecting their daily lives as laypersons. The same year, 1415, Philippa was also present when a girl was given as a nun to the convent.

A few years later, the queen began working more intensely for the good of the abbey. In 1419, she personally wrote letters to the Pope regarding the status of the Birgittine Order, and also engaged her brother, Henry V of England, in the same endeavour.[27] Two years later, and perhaps strengthened by such high-profiled engagements, she asked for a mass to be celebrated daily, for all eternity, for the souls of the king, herself and her parents.[28] The brothers of the monastery later noted that the queen worked in a more notable way than did the king in the business of enhancing the real and symbolic status of the monastery.[29]

Vadstena Abbey and the Claims of the Lancaster House

As seen above, Queen Philippa handled many aspects of her connection to Vadstena Abbey herself and was thus perceived as a person who was unusually devoted to the order. However, the importance of the connection to Vadstena lies beyond her as an individual, and this is evident from the first moment of her queenship in Scandinavia. When the young princess was sent from England to be married in the cathedral in Lund, she was accompanied by a large entourage. Most notable was Henry of Ravensworth, an English knight, who immediately after the wedding headed to Vadstena to establish contact and to assure the brothers and sisters that he intended to establish a monastery of the Birgittine order in England. This was the beginning of several years of work, during which many brothers and sisters from Vadstena were sent to England to establish the new monastery.

The result was Syon Abbey in England, created in 1415, and supported by Henry V. In the memorial book of Vadstena Abbey, there are several entries dealing with the establishment of this English monastery. These entries give the impression that the establishment of Syon Abbey was more important than any of the other new establishments taking place during the fifteenth century. The Birgittine order also established itself in Denmark, Norway, Germany as well as other places, but the creation of a house in England is the only event of this kind that is marked by elaborate ceremonies in the memorial book. In May 1415, seven women and two men left Vadstena Abbey to travel to England and found the new monastery. They were led from Vadstena "with great ceremony", conducted by the Archbishop of Lund, three bishops from Sweden and one from Norway. A large number of knights and high envoys were also present during this public and prestigious event.[30] Indeed, this is the only time that such a ceremony is recorded in the context of founding a new Birgittine abbey. For instance, regarding the foundation of a new abbey on Lolland, Denmark, the same year, there is no record of any participation of high clergy and knights.[31]

The high value placed on the foundation of Syon Abbey is explained by its role in the creation of legitimate claims by Henry V. Saint Birgitta had become a central figure in English political propaganda. In her earliest revelations in the 1340s, the Virgin Mary had suggested a solution to her regarding the conflicts between England and France. The Virgin said that the English royal family had legitimate claims to the throne of France, and suggested a long-term solution whereby the French King Philip VI would adopt the English King Edward III as his son and successor, thus solving the problem without violence. In later versions of this revelation, it was instead noted that the Virgin wished dynastic marriages between the French and the English to solve the issue. Either way, Saint Birgitta's revelations provided the English kings with an important ideological tool to support their claims to France, and by the fifteenth century, Birgitta had come to be perceived as one of England's most important saints. Saint George is another such saint. He was by most accounts a man martyred in what is today Turkey in the fourth century, but was perceived as an English saint by the English in the fifteenth century.[32]

Henry V's use of Saint Birgitta has been analysed by Nancy Bradley Warren. She notes how the Lancastrian kings closed down several other monasteries and gave the funds to the new Syon Abbey. Henry V even provided for it in his will. The founding of Syon took place in 1415, shortly before the war in which Henry emerged victorious at Agincourt. When he returned from battle he was greeted by an enormously lavish ceremony, in which earlier male warrior saints were evoked, but also the Virgin Mary and virgin saints in general.[33] Henry V thus succeeded in linking himself and his victory to the lustre of earlier English saints, but also to Saint Birgitta and the Virgin Mary, two women who symbolically bolstered his claim to the throne of France through his mother's ancestry.

Thus, the emphasis on the Birgittine order in the first half of the fifteenth century was not solely created by Queen Philippa. From the moment of her marriage, a link was established between her native England and the Birgittines of Vadstena Abbey in Sweden. The Abbey and the order were important in many respects and thus constituted a media platform not only for her, but for her father and brother as well. With time, however, Philippa was able to act personally to create her own use of the resource provided by the Birgittines.

Conclusion

Vadstena Abbey surfaced as a media platform for Queen Philippa for several reasons. It was used to propagate claims to legitimate rule, both by pointing to hereditary rights and by establishing moral rights. Through her foundation of an altar and a future burial site, she created a close and highly visible affiliation with the spatial centre of Sweden at the time. She also emphasized the importance of holy women through her commission of works depicting Saint Anne and Saint Mary. The links between England and Scandinavia were underlined even further by the prayers that were to be said every day in Vadstena for herself, her husband and her parents. Her self-chosen burial place, the altar and the masses thus constituted additional memory sites that were meant to last infinitely. Moreover, these media platforms also inscribed her into the community of Christians and the community of the realm, linking her to everyone who contributed to Vadstena Abbey and the Birgittines, even after she was dead.

There must certainly have been aspects of the link between Philippa and Vadstena that were observed by her contemporaries, but that are lost to us today. However, the love and devotion she showed the monastery, not only through gifts and good works but also through her many recurring visits, must have made a profound impression on everyone at the time. When she died in 1430, Philippa was in Vadstena to celebrate Christmas and the New Year.[34] The conversations and the care she shared with the brothers can be seen as subtle and private rituals that also communicated valuable aspects of her power as a public and medially conscious Queen. And because the medieval female saints with whom she aligned herself functioned as mediators between the spiritual and secular worlds even after her death, Queen Philippa of Scandinavia can be said to have functioned as a kind of medieval medium in her own right.

Notes

1. Paul Strohm, *England's Empty Throne: Usurpation and the Language of Legitimation, 1399-1422* (New Haven & London: Yale University Press, 1998).
2. Georges Duby, *The Three Orders* (Chicago: University of Chicago Press, 1980).
3. Anders Fröjmark, *Mirakler och helgonkult: Linköpings biskopsdöme under senmedeltiden* (Uppsala: Uppsala University, 1992). Lars Andersson, *Pilgrimsmärken och vallfart: Medeltida pilgrimskultur i Skandinavien* (Lund: Almqvist & Wiksell International, 1989).
4. Louise Berglund, *Guds stat och maktens villkor: Politiska ideal i Vadstena kloster ca 1370-1470* (Uppsala: Uppsala University, 2003).
5. Asa Briggs & Peter Burke, *A Social History of the Media: From Gutenberg to the Internet* (Cambridge: Polity Press, 2002), p. 1.
6. Ibid., p. 2.
7. Ibid., p. 10.
8. Berglund.
9. Briggs & Burke, pp. 10-11.
10. Alberto Manguel, *A History of Reading* (London: Flamingo, 1997).
11. The gravestone is a copy of the original and dates from the sixteenth century. See Aron Andersson, *Vadstena klosterkyrka*, 2, *Inredning* (Stockholm: Almqvist & Wiksell International, 1983), Robert Bennet, *Vadstena klosterkyrka*, 3, *Gravminnen* (Stockholm: Almqvist & Wiksell International, 1985).
12. Fröjmark, and Lars Andersson.
13. Claes Gejrot (ed), *Vadstenadiariet: Latinsk text med översättning och kommentar* (Stockholm: Samfundet för utgivande av handskrifter rörande Skandinaviens historia, 1996); subsequently referred to as *Diarium Vadstenense*.
14. *Diarium Vadstenense,* no 406, 6 January 1430.
15. In the sources, the location is alternately called "altar" (*Diarium Vadstenense*, no. 374, 27 December 1427, and *Svenskt Diplomatarium*, letter 20990, 14280418), "the queen's chapel" (*Diarium Vadstenense*, no. 698, 29 June 1459), "cross" (*Svenskt Diplomatarium*, letter 20459, 14250325a), and "prebend" (*Svenskt Diplomatarium*, letter 20931, 14271221). It was probably an altar. For *Svenskt Diplomatarium* (subsequently referred to as SD) see, http://www.statensarkiv.se/default.aspx?id=4044.
16. *Diarium Vadstenense,* no 698, 1459.
17. *Diarium Vadstenense,* no 379, 18 May 1427. The bishop of Stavanger, Audun, was installed by the bishops of Linköping, Skara and Växjö.
18. *Diarium Vadstenense,* no 641, 8 January 1454.

19. Mereth Lindgren, "De heliga änkorna: S. Anna-kultens framväxt, speglad i birgittinsk ikonografi", *Konsthistorisk tidskrift* 1990 (1-2), pp. 58-60.
20. SD no. 20459, 25 March 1425.
21. SD no. 20931, 21 December 1427. Issued at Helsingborg.
22. SD no. 20990, 18 April 1428.
23. Lindgren.
24. Katherine J. Lewis, "Becoming a Virgin King: Richard II and Edward the Confessor", in Samantha J.E. Riches & Sarah Salih (eds), *Gender and Holiness: Men, Women and Saints in Late Medieval Europe* (London: Routledge, 2002), p. 88.
25. Eamon Duffy, *The Stripping of the Altars: Traditional Religion in England 1400-1580* (New Haven & London: Yale University Press, 2005), p. 16, 132.
26. Birgitta Fritz, "Kung Magnus Erikssons planer för Vadstena klosterkyrka – och Birgittas", in Steinar Supphellen (ed), *Kongsmenn og krossmenn: Festskrift til Grethe Authén Blom* (Trondheim: Tapir forlag, 1992). Birgitta Fritz, "Vadstena klosterkyrka och kung Magnus testamente 1346", in Per Beskow & Annette Landen (eds), *Birgitta av Vadstena: Pilgrim och profet 1303-1373: En jubileumsbok* (Stockholm: Natur & Kultur, 2003).
27. Hans Cnattingius, *Studies in the Order of St. Bridget of Sweden*, 1, *The Crisis in the 1420s* (Stockholm: Almqvist & Wiksell, 1963).
28. *Diarium Vadstenense*, no. 322, 18 March 1421.
29. *Diarium Vadstenense*, no. 333, 17 June 1422.
30. *Diarium Vadstenense*, no. 254, 21 May 1415.
31. *Diarium Vadstenense*, no. 258, 1415, and no. 268.
32. Samantha J.E. Riches, "St George as a Male Virgin Martyr", in Riches & Salih (eds).
33. Nancy Bradley Warren, "Kings, Saints and Nuns: Gender, Religion and Authority in the Reign of Henry V", *Viator: Medieval and Renaissance Studies* 1999 (30), pp. 308-322.
34. Sven-Bertil Jansson (ed), *Engelbrektskrönikan* (Stockholm: Tiden, 1994).

Royal Bronze

Monarchy and Monuments in the Nineteenth Century

Magnus Rodell

Monuments depicting historical or present royalty were omnipresent phenomena in the monarchical states of nineteenth century Europe. In 1868, a monument dedicated to the late Prince Albert, the husband of Queen Victoria, was inaugurated close to Hyde Park in London.[1] During the last decades of the nineteenth century, hundreds of monuments to Victor Emmanuel II, in Italy, and Wilhelm I, in Germany, were unveiled.[2] In Sweden, the new monarchical dynasty of the Bernadottes became the object of several monumental projects during the 1840s and 1850s.[3] Throughout the nineteenth century, royal monuments constituted a pan-European cultural phenomenon.

At inauguration ceremonies of monuments, royalties could serve a twofold function. On the one hand, as heads of the nation, their presence was seen as a prerequisite, and a symbolic sanction of the inauguration as a solemn, public event. This meaning related back to an older, hierarchical and corporeal society in which the king served as an embodiment of the nation. On the other hand, past or present kings could concurrently be the very object of monumental representation. This was the case for a substantial proportion of the monuments unveiled in Sweden between 1850 and 1900. Even if several of these monuments portrayed former kings, they were at the same time heavily embedded in contemporary processes of modern nation-building.

In the present article, I will mostly focus on the latter function and argue that this kind of royal monument, dedicated to past and present kings, served as a means of mediating monarchy in nineteenth century Sweden. Although my empirical focus is Sweden, the discussion has a general historical relevance, as similar manifestations and monuments, as my introductory examples show, were found in the United Kingdom, Germany, Italy and other European monarchies until the eruption of the Great War. In this period of European history, old monarchies, or new ones, had to deal with growing national sentiments, political radicalism and political and social movements; these were parts of the process of modernization that swept through the Western world during these decades. Thus, mediation became a part of depicting these processes.

Commemorating past and present monarchy could serve varying purposes. In Germany, 1913 became a festive year: A hundred years had passed since the victory at Leipzig, and Wilhelm II celebrated 25 years as monarch. Therefore various celebrations took place throughout the year. Jeffrey R. Smith has shown how several of these events were staged by the Kaiser and his administration in ways that implicitly excluded the German people. Liberals, social democrats as well as right wing nationalists felt excluded and criticized the events for focusing too much on the Kaiser and being too "medieval". In this context, Wilhelm II tried to use the monarchical institution to create legitimacy, but failed.[4] In Gothenburg, the most dynamic trading centre in mid nineteenth century Sweden, a statue of the seventeenth century king Gustavus Adolphus was unveiled in 1854. In speeches and in articles, his peaceful deeds were related to the contemporary liberal agenda of progress through reform. The statue had been initiated by local authorities who greatly supported trade and commerce as a means of progress. In the context of the inauguration, these authorities and the local press actively used specific aspects of the history of the heroic king and the presence of contemporary royalty to sanction their own societal aspirations and visions.

As an artistic expression and a spatial media form, the complexity of the nineteenth century public monument was overlooked for a long time. Within art history, the public monument has generally been seen as a parenthesis between formative epochs such as eighteenth century classicism, early nineteenth century romanticism and early twentieth century modernism. In their traditional, non-radical, non-vanguard style, they were considered not original enough. Being didactic and shaping national identities, the public monument fell outside the main focus of twentieth century art history.[5] Even if brilliant exceptions exist, this is a distinct trend in large parts of twentieth century art historiography.[6] Despite their traditional form and comprehensible inscriptions, the monuments were used as a means of shaping a common history, as well as depicting progress and processes of modernization. To argue that royal monuments during the nineteenth century were solely about celebrating a glorious long gone past, or about sanctioning present day monarchy, would be to take an overly simplified stance.

Just as concepts like "traditional" and "modern" may hinder the sight of art historians and result in an evolutionary historiography, they may also leads us the wrong way if we consider a concept like monarchy to be automatically conservative and traditional. This has of course very often been the case, but new historical insights may be found.[7] This is one of the vital arguments I will develop below. Although the purpose of monuments was to serve as media forms with material durability over time, they were nevertheless deeply imbued with contemporary processes. For example, the inaugurations functioned as temporary, public arenas. Various media actors, politicians, royal individuals and other interest groups made the inaugurations into grand public events, which reached an audience much larger than the one present at the actual inauguration ceremony.

Here, I will analyse the various ways past as well as present monarchs were used in the context of the inaugurations. Royal monuments served as a media form that created and communicated notions about monarchy, the nation, the

Nineteenth century monuments had a didactic purpose. Through their physic presence they should teach certain ideals. Statue of Charles XIV John. *Photo:* Stockholm City Museum.

past, but also notions about the present and the future. As a media form, the monument was part of a wider media landscape that made various visualizations of the royal family available to a broader public. Before discussing two specific statues – Charles XIV John in Stockholm and Gustavus Adolphus in Gothenburg, both erected in 1854 – I will elaborate more generally on monuments as a form of narrating media.

A Spatial Narrating Media Form

Within a cultural history of media, there has been an emphasis on a broader media concept that not only includes traditional media forms such as the press, radio and TV, but also explores spatial media forms such as dioramas, waxworks and monuments.[8] In accordance, I argue that the royal monument can be seen as a spatial media form within the media landscape of the second half of the nineteenth century. In its materially stability, the royal monument functioned as a narrating spatial media form in several different ways.[9] The thousands of monuments unveiled in the western hemisphere between 1848 and the outbreak of World War I can be characterized by certain specific features. *First* they had a didactic purpose. Their vigorous physic presence should stress and teach certain ideals and ideas. The word monument descends from the Latin word "monumentum", which can be related to the verb "monere", which means to remind, to exhort, to teach.[10] To serve a pedagogical purpose, the inscriptions on the monuments were often in the vernacular language.

If monuments are explored as one media form among many, their character is not as ephemeral as the daily paper, the weekly illustrated paper or the diorama, as the monument was meant to last over time, which can be considered a *second* feature. For the contemporary generation as well as for future generations, the monument should inculcate the same message. The fact that it should freeze a certain narrative and hand it down to posterity explains why several monument projects throughout Europe were surrounded by disagreement and outright conflicts. Although monuments were meant to create durability and enforce one narrative, they were interpreted in various ways even at the time they were inaugurated. Sometimes the interpretations clashed, sometimes they just diverged. In the cultural history of monuments, one finds a peculiar relationship between ambiguity and constancy.

A *third* feature designating statues and monuments during the decades around 1900 was that they in most cases conveyed various narratives about the nation. The nation served as an overarching framework through which the statues were ascribed meaning. James E. Young states that: "The matrix of a nation's monuments emplots the story of ennobling events, of triumphs over barbarism, and recalls the martyrdom of those who gave their lives in the struggle for national existence".[11] Looking at monuments and statues inaugurated throughout Europe between 1848 and 1914, heroic narratives related to specific events were reoccurring. Heroic deeds and great sacrifices were not only ascribed kings, but also legendary freedom fighters abiding in the shadows of an almost mythical past.[12]

A *fourth* feature was that the statue, in the context of the inauguration, served as a means of connecting the past, the present and the future. Lewis Mumford has argued that nineteenth century monuments cannot be associated with the idea of progress or modern societal development.[13] However, taking into consideration what was said or written when statues were unveiled, it becomes obvious that various representations of the past were clearly related to the present and pointed out the course for the coming generations. By commemorating heroic deeds of the past, the monument was to inspire and serve as an ideal for future generations. The dynamics between the past, the present and the future was clearly related to the didactic purposes of the monument, and to the nation as an overarching framework. The interplay between varying temporal layers characterized the narratives produced through the inaugurations.[14]

Monuments are spatial and materially consistent means of communication. However, the meanings of a monument are the result of a collaboration between different media forms, which could be seen as the *fifth* characteristic feature. Before any inauguration, programmes informing about the order of the event were published in the local dailies. Sometimes they were also printed separately. Articles in the press informed about the coming event and often about the production of the monument. The ceremonies were followed by extensive reports and articles that often were accompanied by various forms of visual depictions, not least in the illustrated weekly papers that were established from the 1840s onwards. Inaugurations of monuments and statues were extensively covered by various media forms. In addition to programmes, articles in dailies and weekly papers, editors, publishers, poets, singers and playwrights made their various contributions.[15] This plethora of media forms reached a far greater audience than the one that was able to be present at the actual inauguration. The inauguration and its surrounding production of meaning can thus be understood in terms of a media event.[16]

Inventing a Tradition: A New Dynasty in Bronze

In the beginning of November, 1854, the readers of the Stockholm daily *Aftonbladet* were informed about the coming inauguration of the statue of Charles XIV John. Invited royalty and officials were mentioned, the order of the ceremony was published, as were news items from local papers.[17] In *Aftonbladet* and several other Stockholm papers, the readers could also find adverts on new literature. One title that was available in the bookstores of the capital, but also in the provinces, was *Konung Carl XIV Johans historia* (*The History of Charles XIV John*). Alongside a story about "the great king's feats and fates; from the cradle to the grave", the buyer also received a reproduction of the statue.[18] Another publication was entitled *Carl XIV Johan*, and it contained a biographic sketch and an appendix including speeches, letters, and proclamations made by the "the great king". The book also included a portrait and a plate depicting the house in Pau, the French village where the king was born in 1763.[19] On the day of the inauguration, November 4, 1854, the newspapers published articles about the king portrayed in bronze, and the festivities that had taken place.

The equestrian statue of Charles XIV John was inaugurated in November 1854. The statue was a part of giving the new monarchical dynasty of the Bernadottes legitimacy. *Photo:* Stockholm City Museum.

Before exploring these events, we need to go back in time ten years. In mid-April 1844, a month after the death of Charles XIV John, the entrepreneur John Swartz, and 40 of the most prominent among the local bourgeoisie, in the industrial town of Norrköping (160 kilometres southwest of Stockholm), delivered a donation and a written document to the town's local authorities, suggesting that the town erect a statue of the late king. The authorities decided to execute the project and Swartz's document was published in one of the local papers. During the forthcoming weeks, the newspaper informed about various contributions to the statue. Money donations were documented on subscription lists. Alongside bigger contributions from the local bourgeoisie, hundreds of workers, mostly from the local textile industries, donated smaller amounts. The aforementioned paper published lists of the donations and thus created an image that erecting the statue of the late king was an enterprise that people from all walks of society supported, according to their means.[20]

On July 24, 1845, Norrköping was visited by the Queen Dowager Desideria. She was to lay the first stone in erecting the monument. In this ceremony, various local authorities of course took part. The queen dowager was given a trowel in silver with which she put mortar on the first stone.[21] The trowel served as a symbol. In the context of the ceremony and through the presence of the queen dowager, the trowel and the action gave the monument project an official sanction, and the project publicly confirmed its validity. This function is still a vital part of contemporary European royal culture, and is unthinkable without various actions being further legitimized by the media.

In April 1846, the statue was founded at Ferdinand Miller's famous foundry in Munich, and in May a deputation from Norrköping met King Oscar I to proclaim that the statue was completed. At this occasion, Oscar I decided that the unveiling would take place on October 20, the 36th anniversary of Charles XIV John's first steps on Swedish soil. On the solemn day of the inauguration, one of the leaders among the local authorities, John Moselius, held a speech in which he formulated a number of themes that recurred in Stockholm ten years later. Charles XIV John was described as a father of his people and as a surety for national progress. The main purposes of the monument were to remind coming generations about the king's efforts for Sweden and that his deeds should serve as an ideal for the people of the present.[22]

In his speech, Moselius also described the statue. Charles XIV John was not dressed in his "royal robe", because "we wished" to indicate "the hero and the citizen". The king's background shows "us" that he was an ordinary man, "born of bourgeois parents in a cramped hut at the feet of the Pyrenees." By his own efforts and ambitions, he managed to rise to become king. In times of war and misfortunes, the Swedish people found in him a worthy successor. "Fighting for the independence and freedom of Nations", he played a vital role in "restoring peace in Europe". He also made a peaceful union with Norway possible, and during his reign peace was kept in his domains.[23] This was also communicated in the inscription on the statue: "To Charles XIV John, Father of the sister nations, from Oscar I". ("Åt Carl XIV Johan, Brödrafolkens fader, af Oscar I").[24] Depicted as a citizen, fighting against Napoleon, Charles XIV John was related to the civic culture that constituted a vital part of the heritage of the French revolution. Within a narrative of revolutions, war and political change, the work of the coming monarch was ascribed meaning.

The crucial components of this narrative recurred in Stockholm in 1854. At this occasion, *Aftonbladet* stated that the homage that Oscar I had dedicated to his father was doubly motivated, as Charles XIV John had earned his crown, not through descent, but through his personal merits. Oscar I's arrangement of the equestrian statue was also complemented in the article. It is not the king over two realms who was "conjured up in the metal". As in Norrköping, no royal attributes were used, and the king was dressed in the warring dress he preferred to wear; the costume in which "we met princely elegance" and the way most Swedes remember him. The writer stated that "we" prefer to see him as "the world renowned marshal of France, the son of a new society", the brave ravishing genius, "in the moment he entered his capital to be".[25]

In creating the statue, the artist Bengt Erland Fogelberg had had the judgement to use the "wonderful romance" that dominated the early life of Charles XIV John. In front of the statue, the observer was immediately brought to the valleys that saw the birth of the hero, to the changing scenes of the revolution, where the young republican soldier showed courage and resolution, but also "a noble heart, and a true humanity, to all the various walks of Europe where he brought new glory to the weapons of the French republic".[26] In Norrköping in 1846, as well as in Stockholm in 1854, although the initiators were different, there was an emphasis on the socially mobile soldier from a simple background who became a general in the armies of Napoleon, and then switched sides to eventually become king, and the first in a new European monarchical dynasty.

One might be tempted to argue that this narrative was solely about the past. But it needs to be situated within the reign of Oscar I. In Swedish historiography he has been described as a liberal king. In contrast to the repressive years that dominated, above all, Charles XIV John's last decade as king. In Sweden, as well as in other parts of Europe, radical elements within the liberal establishment were to some extent marginalized after the revolutions in 1848 and 1849. Nevertheless, the late 1840s and the 1850s were characterized by liberal reform, although the liberal culture in the 1850s was of a more moderate character.[27] The initiator behind the equestrian statue was Oscar I, and it was thus far the most expensive statue ever erected in Sweden.[28] Erecting the statue was a part of giving the new dynasty legitimacy. With this in mind, narratives of a self-made man and a revolutionary hero served those means a great deal better than an aging king, reluctant about societal change and reform. In this indirect way, the production of meaning at the inauguration was also related to the political conditions in contemporary Sweden.[29]

More thorough descriptions of the statue were presented in other articles, as well as brochures. Directly after the inauguration, the brochure *Carl XIV Johan: Några minnesblad (Charles XIV John: Some Memorial Pages)* was published by one of the bigger publishing houses in Stockholm. Many of the texts that had been published in newspapers, above all the official daily *Post- och Inrikes Tidningar*, were reprinted in the brochure. It also contained an image of the statue. The same texts circulated through different media forms. All the various components served the overarching purpose of mediation. The descriptions were very detailed, as if they were meant to visualize the order of the event for those not present.

The story of establishing the statue was presented, as was its physical appearance. The dailies and the brochure stated that the equestrian statue of Charles XIV John was the sixth "colossal" public statue in Stockholm. The statue of Gustavus Vasa was inaugurated in 1774 and it was followed by statues of Gustavus Adolphus in 1796, Gustavus III in 1808 and Charles XIII in 1821. The statue of Birger jarl, the founder of Stockholm, was unveiled on October 21, 1854, just two weeks before the statue of Charles XIV John.[30] The new statue was situated among the others and made a part of Stockholm's geography of monuments, depicting and communicating various aspects of Swedish history, and creating a pantheon of past kings. Through the newspapers the readers could take part in the ceremonies on the inauguration day. Informed about the other monuments (four of them royal monuments), the public was subsequently served the possibility to stroll around the city to see the old monuments as well as the two new ones. The ephemeral newspapers drew public attention to more lasting spatial media forms. The public should not only read about the monuments, it should also physically experience them. Even if it was not explicitly formulated, seeing the new monument the observer could hence testify to the fact that it was the most glorious of them all.

Gustavus Adolphus as a Liberal Reformer

Using a past king as a means of inscribing the relevance of a political agenda became even more obvious in Gothenburg, where a statue of Gustavus Adolphus was erected on November 18, 1854. In 1845, a man among the local authorities suggested that Gothenburg should erect a statue of Gustavus Adolphus.[31] In one article, the local daily gave the project a wider anchorage. People visiting Gothenburg will, according to the newspaper, see that the town has changed. Old ramparts have been demolished, pavements have been put into order, beautiful, privately owned houses have been built and a botanical garden set up. The construction of an exchange building had begun which "without any doubt will become one of the distinguished buildings of the city". And decisions had been taken to let Gothenburg be lighted by gas.[32]

The newspaper described a modernization of the town with all its various demands on city planning. The coronet on this work would be the erection of a statue, in "a colossal size", of the city founder.[33] The statue would be the culmination of the transformation of the city and serve as a testimony to its bustle and progress. The material solidity and future presence of a statue might seem to be in glaring contrast to this rhetoric of bustle and progress. However, the statue project can be interpreted as a way of creating an enduring symbol of the origins of the town in a time of transformation and expansion. Erecting and inaugurating the statue of Gustavus Adolphus should not be seen as a passive mark for overall societal progress, but rather as one of several means of shaping change and progress.[34] The rhetoric of peaceful development and change was to be given a historical foundation when the statue was inaugurated nine years later, in the autumn of 1854.

The statue was unveiled in the presence of Crown Prince Charles, military units, the civilian corpses and estates of the town, invited guests and a 120-man-strong choir.[35] The day before the inauguration, a long article was published in *Göteborgs Handels- och Sjöfarts-Tidning*. In the article, attention was directed to the fact that Gustavus Adolphus' military achievements often had been overemphasized, while his peaceful pursuits had rarely been taken into consideration. Despite the wars, he worked for the peaceful development of the kingdom. He safeguarded the continuing activity of Uppsala University through a large donation. Gustavus Adolphus' contributions to education also entailed the founding of several grammar schools throughout the Swedish empire. Furthermore, he made important contributions to the constitutional field. He also worked for Sweden's industrial development. The iron industry was improved, as were textile mills. Roads were enhanced and several cities founded, among them Gothenburg.[36]

The "professions of peace" that were discussed – the encouragement of science and education, the improvement of the constitution, industrial expansion and the development of the infrastructure – were all on the contemporary agenda of reform liberals. In the article, continuity between Gustavus Adolphus' peaceful activity and the commercially booming Gothenburg of the 1850s was formulated. The aims of contemporary liberals permeated the narrative of Gustavus Adolphus' peaceful endeavours produced in the context of the inauguration. Contemporary economic reformism was presented as a struggle for freedom against old corporative structures. Reform liberals in Gothenburg used specific parts of the history of Gustavus Adolphus to promote their own kind of politics.

This narrative recurred in the way the statue was described. *Post- och Inrikes Tidningar* wrote that the sculptor presented the king the way he looked in his prime when he led Sweden towards a brighter future. The statue referred to the moment when Gustavus Adolphus, standing on the Otterhälle cliff, pointed with his right hand to where the city should be established.[37] The peaceful deeds of Gustavus Adolphus had a vital importance, and were identified with and formulated through mid-nineteenth century liberalism. The past was not only a source of great memories and military honour. It was also used within the framework of contemporary political ambition and future expansion. The clear continuity between Gustavus Adolphus' peaceful achievements and trade expansion in the Gothenburg of the 1850s was brought to the fore.

Conclusion

Naturally, arguing that the mediation of monarchy in the mid-nineteenth century was characterized by narratives of progress and future prospects does not mean that the past was absent. Historical events and processes were omnipresent. However, relating to my general argument, they cannot be separated from the situation in which they were formulated, nor from the future to which they were related. It also leads us the wrong way if we consider a concept like monarchy to be automatically conservative. One of the most famous "heroic kings" – Gustavus Adolphus – as well as the first king in the new monarchical dynasty – Charles XIV John – were both related to contemporary conditions in the context of the inauguration. Charles XIV John was described as the son of the revolution, a republican soldier, a self-made man – this narrative being related to the dramatic events in the beginning of the century. It also had a wider resonance than the narrative about the conservative, aging king, and corresponded more clearly to the overarching liberal culture of the 1850s. And Gustavus Adolphus, on the statue, pointing to where the new town should be built, was turned into a reform liberal, supporting and investing in enterprises similar to those of the trading classes in Gothenburg in the 1850s.

Various media forms were used in the process of ascribing the monarchs with these characteristics. Through newspaper articles, poems, pamphlets, books, adverts and other media items, the unveilings were turned into media events that reached a wide audience. As an informal institution, the inauguration of statues in mid-nineteenth century Sweden and Europe would not have been possible without various media.[38] Easily accessible media forms made the unveilings into popular events, where monarchy and media were intertwined.

During the second half of the nineteenth century, it is also possible to view monuments as spatial media forms that represented a range of narratives, structured according to certain characteristics. The didactic purpose of the statues of Charles XIV John and Gustavus Adolphus was clearly brought to the fore. Charles XIV John's heroic deeds should serve as an ideal for all Swedes. *Post- och Inrikes Tidningar* wrote that the statue served as an "inescapable" and "permanent request" about all the "virtues" needed to create "a great man's imperishable reputation".[39] The physical presence of the statue made this remembrance possible. In the case of Gustavus Adolphus, it was his peaceful pursuits and activities that were to inspire contemporary generations, as well as the generations to come.

Statues could serve various agendas and ideas, but generally the statues inaugurated between 1848 and 1914 were a means of creating and inscribing national sentiments. The deeds of past kings were situated in a framework of contemporary nation-building, and they were made into symbols through which notions and ideas of nation-hood could be promulgated. Another seminal feature was the interplay between the past, the present and the future. In Gothenburg in 1854, speeches and articles linked the deeds of the past king to the contemporary conditions in Gothenburg and Sweden. If complete freedom of trade were realized, Sweden would experience ever-increasing progress and development. In formulating this, the dynamic interplay between the past, the present and the future played an important role. As discussed above, the monument was communicated in and through other media forms and thus became an inseparable part of the media culture.

In the context of the inaugurations, it is also important to remember that royalties present on the occasion served as the main attractions. People participating were probably not only interested in seeing the statue of a historical king unveiled, but also in the presence of the monarchical dynasty. Throughout the course of the nineteenth century, monarchy became a vital part of public culture. Inaugurations of monuments, the opening of railroads and big exhibitions were unthinkable without the presence of royalty – a role still played by the European monarchies today.

Notes

1. Chris Brooks, *The Albert Memorial: The Prince Consort National Memorial, Its History, Context, and Conversation* (New Haven: Yale University Press, 2000).

2. See for example David Atkinson & Denis Cosgrove, "Urban Rhetoric and Embodied Identities: City, Nation, and Empire at the Vittorio Emanuele II Monument in Rome, 1870-1945", *Annals of the Association of American Geographers* 1998 (1), and Abigail Green, *Fatherlands: Statue-Building and Nationhood in Nineteenth Century Germany* (Cambridge: Cambridge University Press, 2001).

3. See for example Magnus Rodell, "Att gjuta en nation: Om statyinvigningar i Sverige på 1800-talet", unpublished MA-thesis, Department of History of Science and Ideas (Uppsala, 1996); Bengt Järbe, *Stockholms statyer* (Stockholm: Byggförl./Kultur, 1997), pp. 64-66, and Solfrid Söderlind, "Den leuchtenbergska kopplingen", *Artes: Tidskrift för litteratur, konst och musik* 1997 (4), pp. 30-43.

4. Jeffrey R. Smith, "The Monarchy versus the Nation: The 'Festive Year' 1913 in Wilhelmine Germany", *German Studies Review*, 2002 (2), pp. 257-274, especially pp. 264-270.

5. See for example Lars Berggren, *Giordano Bruno på Campo dei Fiori: Ett monumentprojekt i Rom 1876-1889* (Lund: Wallin & Dalholm, 1991), and Magnus Rodell, *Att gjuta en nation: Statyinvigningar och nationsformering i Sverige vid 1800-talets mitt* (Stockholm: Natur & Kultur, 2002).

6. In Sweden, the most notable exception is Allan Ellenius's pioneering study *Den offentliga konsten och ideologierna: Studier över verk från 1800- och 1900-talen* (Stockholm: Almqvist & Wicksell, 1971).

7. Compare Mats Jönsson, "'Den kungliga skölden': Per Albin Hansson, Gustaf V och medierna 1940", in Mats Jönsson & Pelle Snickars (eds), *Medier och politik: Om arbetarrörelsens mediestrategier under 1900-talet* (Stockholm: SLBA, 2007), pp. 195-196.

8. See for example Anders Ekström, Solveig Jülich & Pelle Snickars, "Inledning: I mediearkivet", Ekström, Jülich & Snickars, (eds), *1897: Mediehistorier kring Stockholmsutställningen* (Stockholm: SLBA, 2006), pp. 7 and 16-17.

9. I discuss monuments as a narrating medium more extensively in "Fallna soldater och fortifikationer i vildmarken: Det ryska hotet och medielandskapet kring 1900", in Leif Dahlberg & Pelle Snickars (eds), *Berättande i olika medier* (Stockholm: SLBA, 2008), pp. 85-89.

10. Berggren, p. 19.

11. James E. Young, *The Texture of Memory: Holocaust Memorials and Meaning* (New Haven & London: Yale University Press, 1993), p. 2

12. See also Rodell, *Att gjuta en nation*, pp. 218-219.

13. Lewis Mumford, *The Culture of Cities* (New York: Harcourt, Brace and Company, 1938), pp. 433-440.

14. See also Rodell, *Att gjuta en nation*, pp. 45-46.

15. Compare ibid., pp. 172-175.

16. See also, Patrik Lundell, "The Medium is the Message: The Media History of the Press", *Media History*, 2008 (1), p. 5.

17. *Aftonbladet* 3 November 1854.

18. Advert, *Aftonbladet* 1 November 1854.

19. Ibid.

20. Knut Wichman, *Från Karl Johanstidens Norrköping* (Göteborg: Föreningen Gamla Norrköping, 1957), p. 18. Handlingar ang Karl XIV Johans-monumentet 1844-1848, F 4, Norrköpings stadsarkiv.

21. Erik Krigström, *Swartz – en släkt i Norrköping: Stadshistorisk utställning 1959-1960* (Norrköping: Norrköpings museum, 1959), p. 16.

22. Handlingar ang Karl XIV Johans-monumentet 1844-1848, F 4, Norrköpings stadsarkiv. *Tal inför H. M. Konung Oscar 1:ste före Aftäckningen af Högsts. Konung Carl XIV Johans Bildstod i Norrköping d. 20 October 1846* (Norrköping, 1846).

23. Ibid.

24. "Carl Johans Torg och Stod", *Post- och Inrikes Tidningar* 3 November 1854.

25. "Stockholm, den 4 Nov.", *Aftonbladet* 4 November 1854.

26. Ibid.

27. See for example Alf Kjellén, *Sociala idéer och motiv hos svenska författare under 1830- och 1840-talen*, II, *(1844-1848): Från patriarkalism till marxism* (Stockholm, 1950), pp. 16-23; Åke Holmberg, *Skandinavismen i Sverige: Vid 1800-talets mitt (1843-1863)* (Göteborg, 1946), pp. 88-89 and 93; Eric Johannesson, "August Blanche, den ädle folkvännen", in Kurt Johannisson et al., *Heroer på offentlighetens scen: Politiker och publicister i Sverige 1809-1914* (Stockholm: Tiden, 1987), p. 107.

28. Solfrid Söderlind, *Porträttbruk i Sverige 1840-1865: En funktions- och interaktionsstudie* (Stockholm: Carlssons, 1993), p. 340.

29. The making of the new dynasty during the reign of Charles XIV John is discussed and analysed in Mikael Alm & Britt-Inger Johansson (eds), *Scripts of Kingship: Essays on Bernadotte and Dynastic Formulation in an Age of Revolution* (Uppsala: Department of History, 2008).

30. *Carl XIV Johan: Några minnesblad af den 4 November 1854: Med en afbildning af statyen* (Stockholm: Albert Bonniers förlag, 1854), p. 8.

31. C.R.A. Fredberg, *Det gamla Göteborg: Lokalhistoriska skildringar, personalia och kulturdrag*, II (Göteborg, 1921-1922), p. 558.

32. "Götheborg", *Göteborgs Handels- och Sjöfarts-Tidning* 6 June 1845.

33. Ibid.

34. This is also discussed in Magnus Rodell, *Att gjuta en nation*, pp. 51-52.

35. *Post- och Inrikes Tidningar* 18 November 1854.

36. "Den 17 November", *Göteborgs Handels- och Sjöfarts-Tidning* 17 November 1854; signature G-a., *Minnes-Verser i anledning af Gustaf Adolfs Statyens aftäckande den 18 November 1854* (Göteborg, 1854).

37. "Gustaf-Adolfs-festen i Götheborg, i dag lördag", *Post- och Inrikes Tidningar* 18 November 1854.

38. Concerning the inauguration as a form of institution, see Magnus Rodell "Teknikens heroer: Pansarskepp och ångturbiner som ett svenskt kulturarv", in Peter Aronsson & Magdalena Hillström (eds), *Kulturarvets dynamik: Det institutionaliserade kulturarvets förändringar* (Linköping: Linköping University, 2005), pp. 117-118.

39. "Stockholm: Carl-Johans-festen", *Post- och Inrikes Tidningar* 4 November 1854.

Pressing the Centre of Attention
Three Royal Weddings and a Media Myth

Kristina Widestedt

Society, whether we prefer to call it global, national, or local, is imbued with mass media – the culture of the twenty-first century is a media culture. People can express and receive their experiences through digital media, fulfil their needs for information as well as friendship through interactive media, and eagerly explore new ways of being constantly connected to the media flow. Media as a means of communication are undisputedly central in contemporary culture. This centrality creates an unarticulated sense of the importance of communication media to modern society as such: as a *society* with shared values and norms, and as a *modern* society with all the possibilities and promises of market capitalism and political liberalism. In fact, the news media's most persistent self-image draws heavily on the close connection between democracy and the Western variety of a free press, to the extent that the state of the press more often than not is regarded as indicative of the state of democracy in a nation or a region.[1] Admittedly, this high regard for the democratic functions of journalism and the press is expressed not only by journalists and media companies, but also by internationally renowned scholars such as Jürgen Habermas, whose theory of the public sphere laid a solid philosophical foundation for advocating the necessity – and the centrality – of media in democratic societies.[2] But why should we find this line of thought credible? And when did it first appear?

In his book *Media Rituals*, Nick Couldry elaborates extensively on what he calls "the myth of the mediated centre". This myth is based on two assumptions. Firstly, the assumption that there is in fact a natural symbolic centre in society, the values and events of which we should all, as citizens, be familiar with. Secondly, the assumption that the news media, as our representatives, have legitimate access to that centre, and that this serves a necessary social purpose. The myth of the mediated centre, accordingly, tells us that each and every one of us is dependent on the mass media to obtain knowledge about the central values and important events in our society. Alternative ways of communication are more or less ruled out by this myth. The idea of the social centre being a mediated centre is itself a news media construction, and as citizens – in the periphery, not in the centre of media attention – we are unwittingly made to understand and accept not only the importance of being informed of what goes on in the centre, but also that this information can be provided only by the news media. In Couldry's words:

> The idea that society has a centre helps naturalise the idea that we have, or need, media that 'represent' that centre; media's claims for themselves that they are society's 'frame' help naturalise the idea, underlying countless media texts, that there is a social 'centre' to *be* re-presented to us.[3]

Thus, the myth of the mediated centre does not tell us that news media are the symbolic, cultural, political or whatever centre of society, but it does tell us that news media encircle this centre like the walls of a medieval city, that they grant themselves the right to keep this centre under constant surveillance and to administer all communication, in both directions, between the centre and the periphery outside. Couldry plants the myth of the mediated centre firmly within the contemporary context of today's society, where the media are omnipresent and even omnipotent. However, taking the constructed character of this myth seriously, it should be possible to trace its origin to a certain period in time – to deconstruct and reconstruct the myth of the mediated centre as a historical product, and to analyse how the social centre is mediated at different stages in time.

Provided that there is in fact one predominating centre of power in society, the news media (in any modern sense of this term) have always regarded it their responsibility to cover that centre in one way or another. The head of state usually takes on the task of personifying the national power centre, for more or less symbolic reasons. Today, national centres of power tend to be represented as synonymous with the actual buildings that symbolise the concentrated leadership of politics – the White House, 10 Downing Street, the Kremlin. The Swedish equivalent of this is Rosenbad, the Government Offices. Historically, however, the national power centre of Sweden has without doubt been the Royal Castle. In spite of the fact that the Swedish monarchy was finally depoliticized in 1974 (a process that started in the nineteenth century), King Carl XVI Gustaf and the royal family continue to be represented as if they were part of our national centre of power, and royal family occasions still take on their traditional character of media events. The centre of political power – government – seems to be something quite distinct from the centre of symbolic power – the monarchy.

In Search of the Centre

The historical development of the myth of the mediated centre is admittedly a far-reaching object of empirical analysis, almost impossible to grasp. In order to reduce the scope to a reasonable level, while still maintaining analytical consistency throughout the study, I have chosen to examine press material from three Swedish royal weddings – in 1888, 1932 and 1976, respectively. The analysis covers visual as well as verbal reporting, from the daily and weekly press. The papers selected are three dailies – *Aftonbladet, Dagens Nyheter* and *Svenska Dagbladet* – and two weeklies – *Idun* (1888) and *Svensk Damtidning* (1932 and 1976).

The first wedding, between Prince Oscar and the noble Ebba Munck, took place in Bournemouth, UK, on 15 March 1888. The dailies published during 14-31 March were studied, and the weekly *Idun* during January through March (13 issues). The total number of journalistic items concerning the royal wedding was 59 (whereof eight in *Idun*), and the visuals – exclusively in *Idun* – were seven. The second wedding, between Prince Gustaf Adolf and Princess Sibylla, was held in Coburg, Germany, on 19 (civic marriage) and 20 (church ceremony) October, 1932. The dailies published during 16-24 October were studied, along with the wedding issue (no. 44) of *Svensk Damtidning*. All in all, the number of journalistic items reporting this wedding was 45 (whereof 15 in *Svensk Damtidning*), and the visual representations totalled 107 (whereof 45 in *Svensk Damtidning*). The third and final wedding, between King Carl XVI Gustaf and Ms Silvia Sommerlath, was celebrated in Stockholm, Sweden, on 19 June 1976. The dailies for 18-20 June and the wedding issue (no. 26) of *Svensk Damtidning* were included in the study, where 134 journalistic items reporting the wedding were found (14 of these in *Svensk Damtidning*) and 238 visuals (74 of these in *Svensk Damtidning*).

This schematic overview reveals an immense increase in the use of visuals, and also an increasing – as well as a more concentrated – news media coverage of royal weddings generally. Mainly due to technical developments during the twentieth century that sped up the photographic publication process, the later observation periods can be much more limited than the first, and still cover the bulk of the wedding ceremony reports. Due to the immense increase in journalistic output during the twentieth century, speculations and contextualizations produced well in advance of the wedding are only included in connection with the 1888 event.

Obtaining more detailed information from the material demands a closer analysis of themes and elements in texts and visuals. We can easily deepen our understanding of the wedding reports through a couple of straightforward research questions: In what ways are the relations between royalties, citizens and media (centre, periphery and media) depicted and constructed in texts and visuals? And how does journalism report and/or reflect on its own participation in the royal weddings?

1888: A Marriage across Social Borders

The engagement between Prince Oscar, second son of King Oscar II, and the noble Ebba Munck, lady-in-waiting to Crown Princess Victoria (spouse of the future King Gustavus V), caused a turmoil in Swedish high society. Male members of the royal house were not allowed to marry beneath their rank, and

Ebba Munck, in spite of her noble lineage, was considered "a woman of the people". In order for this marriage to be possible at all, Prince Oscar had to produce a formal, written request to the king (his father), asking for permission to marry the woman he loved and to denounce his right to the throne along with his royal titles and privileges. This letter, as well as the king's formal letter of consent, was printed *verbatim* in the press, where a considerable interest in the future legal position of the prince was apparent.[4]

The formal and social difficulties surrounding the union of Prince Oscar and Ebba Munck endowed the wedding reports with an unmistakably romantic flavour, reminiscent of old folk tales about pure-hearted princes falling in love with beautiful but poor girls:

> ... one of the fair maidens of the court ... has won a King's son ... in spite of prejudice and paragraphs she won as her husband the man her heart has chosen ... her gentle being ... her warm and full heart ... she, whose beauty, amiability and other characteristics have attracted a prince's attention and captured his heart ... does well deserve the happiness bestowed upon her ...

> ... a member of the Swedish royal house ... the young prince ... has given up the velvet cloak and the princely crown ... has declined the prospect of glory and power ... generally admired and loved for his modest personality and his humane openness ... on his way to winning lasting popularity ...[5]

The wedding ceremony in St Stephen's Church, Bournemouth, was described in vivid detail in the daily papers as well as in the weekly magazine. Additionally, the magazine presented an exclusive woodcut depicting the ceremony in the choir.

The readers are clearly imagined as royal subjects, with subordinate positions on the social ladder. Vaguely gendered in the daily press, the audience is explicitly addressed as female in the magazine. A considerable part of the dailies' reporting consists of the rendering of telegrams sent to the newlyweds from different educational and military associations or civic organizations all over Sweden. This is a representational practice that supposedly serves an integrative function across regions and social positions, and actively includes the male population in the tributes. The inclusive mode unites the papers and the people in heartfelt exclamations, such as, "Warm and sincere congratulations from the people of Sweden to the young prince and his bride!" or "we are convinced that all our female readers join us in cordially wishing the newly engaged couple good luck".[6]

Another prominent trait in the reporting is the consumerist perspective towards the audience. Alongside advertisements selling event-related commercial objects such as plaster busts, paintings and pictures of Ebba Munck or the bridal couple, the papers devote considerable space to two varieties of self-advertising. One is the frequent reference to the presence of numerous international papers and journalists at the wedding, indicating the general news value of the event. Another is the extensive and competitive promotion of exclusive visuals, indicating the 'must-have factor' of the issue in question:

> On the occasion of Prince Oscar's engagement to miss Ebba Munck, this issue is published today Monday instead of Friday. We have undertaken this change so that *Idun* may have the opportunity, before any other paper, to present their honoured female readers with the very newest portrait of the day. It is produced in the atelier of the court photographer Gösta Florman and cut in wood by Mr W. Meyer.[7]

Notable here are the status-signalling title "court photographer" (which adds a touch of *grandeur* to the magazine) and the almost explosive news value of the portrait of the bride-to-be, which is believed shortly to appear in many other papers. All *Idun*'s seven visuals on the occasion of this wedding are put forward as exclusive originals. The most promoted illustrations appear in number 12, and are referred to in a special appendix numbered 11 ½:

> This week's issue of *Idun*, intended to be a festive issue on the occasion of Prince Oscar's marriage, cannot be published until the beginning of next week, since several illustrations, manufactured especially for *Idun* by a most distinguished foreign illustration company, have not reached us in time due to severe weather conditions. [...] The festive issue will contain a number of illustrations, among them the actual wedding ceremony in St Stephen's Church in Bournemouth (exquisite woodcut) etc., etc.[8]

The papers' apparent wish to be connected with cutting-edge technology is perfectly consistent with modern journalism's occupation with "the new", "the current", and "the very latest".[9] By permitting reporters and photographers to take part in and technologically reproduce this royal wedding ceremony, the Bernadottes support the desire for technological modernity. At the same time, however, traditional elements of the event are put forward, such as the Swedish queen's ceremonial arrival at the church, which is described in respectful detail by two of the papers.[10]

The use of cutting-edge information technology notwithstanding, journalism positions itself within the bourgeois private sphere rather than in the Habermasian public sphere by allowing the images of the newlywed couple to acquire the status of private family pictures, and by depicting their wedding as if it were just as important to remember as a wedding within one's own family. In the extensive wedding reports, the royalties are in fact not primarily constructed as power holders or sovereigns, but rather as members of the readers' (extended) family, well in accordance with the traditional view of the king and queen as father and mother of the nation. What is interesting here, however, is how journalism takes on the role of this family's central figure, the inquisitive and well-informed aunt or uncle who knows everything about everyone and is thrilled to share this with absolutely anyone who cares to listen.

Even though this constructed familiarity indicates a clear intent to build a strong relationship between royalties, subjects and media, the centre/periphery model does not quite apply in late nineteenth century Sweden. The organization of society emerging in the 1888 wedding reports is more hierarchically than centrally oriented, with the king on top and his subjects beneath him, and the news media blend into and strengthen this hierarchy by accepting the role of communicator between top and bottom, from the ruler to the ruled. The papers studied here pride themselves on being given access to the wedding ceremonies and thereby having the opportunity to bask in the glory of the royal personages, but this is presented as a privilege gracefully bestowed on the media by royal benevolence, not as mandatory democratic procedure. This is a very important difference from today's naturalized notion of the mediated social centre, where every major event is preceded and followed by countless exclusive media occasions such as press conferences and press reports, to the extent that the organization and management of media discourse at times seems even more important than the organization of the event itself.

The journalism of 1888 obviously predates the myth of the mediated centre, and consequently it describes a different society, a society in which the news media's role as primary channels of information and formers of opinion could still be equalled by family and friends. However, journalism does possess a certain social status, acquired partly through its graciously sanctioned, physical presence at the royal wedding, and partly through its outspoken use of the latest technical equipment, symbolizing the rapid progress of industrialist society.

1932: A Blue-Blooded Wedding

The wedding of Prince Gustaf Adolf, eldest grandson of King Gustavus V, to the German Princess Sibylla of Saxe-Coburg-Gotha was in many ways a classic royal wedding, knitting more closely together the family ties of the royal houses of Europe. Accordingly, one of the most striking elements in the press reports from Coburg is the verbal and visual parading of innumerable royalties with a considerable variety of more or less complicated titles and origins. The media's preoccupation with royal and ex-royal titles and family ties reflects the turmoil on the European continent in the interwar period, when old nations fell apart and new nations and ethnic communities were consolidated or strove for independence.

Another striking element in the reports is the parading of Nazi uniforms – only a couple of days before the royal wedding, the city of Coburg hosted celebrations of the ten-year anniversary of the SA (*Sturmabteilung*), and made Adolf Hitler an honorary Coburg citizen. Add to this that the mayor, who led the civil marriage ceremony, was a uniformed member of the NSDAP (although dressed in civilian clothes during the ceremony), and that Princess Sibylla's father, Grand Duke Carl Eduard, had arranged for SA and SS (*Schutzstaffeln*) soldiers to assist the ordinary police force during the festivities, and the settings of the wedding gradually take on their particular and time-bound appearance.

In spite of the typical fairy-tale motive of "handsome young prince marries beautiful young princess", the fairy-tale narrative is almost completely absent in the reports from the Coburg wedding, and the renderings of the royal protagonists are rather impersonal and not familiar in the same way as they were in 1888. Because the wedding takes place in Germany and not in Sweden, the hooraying and flag-waving citizens in the streets are not Swedish subjects but inhabitants of Coburg. This is, of course, one reason that nationalist-royalist sentiment does not quite present itself in the media reports, despite the elevation and strengthening of the Swedish royal family that was undoubtedly achieved by this marriage. Rather, the Swedish news media establish a clear difference between the two countries by placing the wedding within a specifically German setting – mainly made up of *Hochzeit-Bier und Würstchen, Stahlhelme* and swastika banners – thereby disregarding the age-old family ties between Swedish and German royalties. More than anything, the Coburg wedding is represented as a grand spectacle, and the press invites Swedish readers to watch and be amazed at this predominantly visual event.

The reports from this wedding combine two familiar journalistic discourses: on the one hand the traditionalist discourse, stressing history, dynasties, lineage and heritage, and on the other hand the modernist discourse, stressing the rapidity, accuracy and complexity of (media) technology. The obvious fascination with cameras, film cameras and microphones constitutes a parallel discourse to the wedding reports. A headline from one of the dailies, "Gustavus Adolphus expresses his gratitude on 30 metres of sound-film"[11], demonstrates how these discourses are united into a story of the merging of tradition and modernity, of history and progress. Actually, it is not easy to tell which part of the headline is the most important, "Gustavus Adolphus expresses his gratitude" or "on 30 metres of sound-film".

The sound-film event appears in all four papers, and contains several elements of interest to this study. It begins with an American company, Fox Movietone, filming a brief interview with the prince at an occasion when neither the German nor the Swedish filmmakers had their camera equipments ready. A little later, however, the Swedes and the Germans join their film forces and manage to persuade the prince to express his gratitude for the presents and congratulations. His speech and the consecutive dialogue with the film photographers are extensively quoted in three of the papers, and the fourth (the evening paper *Aftonbladet*) contains an interview with the Swedish filmmakers. The prince's speech is 'reviewed' by a German film technician, who says that the prince has "a splendid sound-film voice" and would be a great success in the film business.[12] As a result, the prince transcends the traditionalist royal discourse and enters the discourse of technological modernity, the realm of the media. The merging of these two discourses is also made visible in some of the photographs from Coburg, where the journalistic thrill of achieving a kind of technological domination over the royals is almost tangible.

The photograph (from *Svensk Damtidning*) is captioned "the bridal couple under press photographers' camera fire", and shows the newlyweds entering the courtyard through an archway in the far left of the image. Photographers with camera equipments are surrounding the courtyard, kneeling behind the royal Mercedes or crowding in thorny rose bushes in order to get their pictures of the royal couple. Obviously, the gathering of members of the international

Brudparet i pressfotografernas kameraeld.

Prince Gustavus Adolphus of Sweden and Princess Sibylla of Saxe-Coburg-Gotha meet the international press photographers and film crews in the courtyard of the Alte Veste, Coburg, after their civic marriage ceremony. *Svensk Damtidning* 29 October 1932.

press corps in Coburg possesses considerable news value in itself; this is but one of many similar images, depicting the interaction between media and royalties. The frequent military metaphors in the articles – "cannonades of camera shots", "battalions of filmmakers and photographers beleaguering Coburg Castle", "murdering fire from the photographers' batteries" – imply that there is a sort of battle going on. Evidently, journalism is at war with royalty, and possibly, this war is about control of the social centre. Pushing the interpretation a little further, the royal couple is not in fact the centre of attention in this photographic rendering. Rather, the viewer's gaze is drawn to the empty segment of courtyard occupying the lower central part of the image. Arguably, this void highlights the symbolic focus of this battle: the social centre lies vacant, waiting for its occupants. What we see in the visuals and texts from Coburg is actually the scaffolding of the myth of the mediated centre, the machinery of the journalistic working process laid bare for everyone to see and admire – and in due course legitimize.

When it comes to the relations between royals, media and audience, the earlier hierarchical organization of society now seems to be approaching the centre/periphery model, and rather than satisfying the royals' demands for respect and subordination, the media increasingly strive to simultaneously create and satisfy a public demand for rapid and stable access to newsworthy events, such as royal weddings. However, the royals also take advantage of the new media technology, thereby strengthening their position in the national centre. The centre is contested, power relations are unstable – but citizens/audiences are unmistakably being pushed towards the periphery of society.

1976: The People's Royal Wedding

In 1976, 30-year-old King Carl XVI Gustaf married tourist hostess Silvia Sommerlath from Heidelberg, West Germany. They had met during the Olympic Games in Munich in 1972, when Carl Gustaf was still crown prince, and managed to keep their relationship a secret for almost four years. At the time of their wedding, the Swedish papers were teeming with fairy-tale narratives, Cinderella-style, about the ordinary girl who fell in love with a king and won the love of his people. Apart from the enormous extent of the press coverage, the reports from this wedding are noteworthy in two respects: Collective national(ist) sentiments are uninhibitedly evoked, and the central role of national as well as international news media in this event is emphasized and taken for granted. A few headlines from the material exemplify these tendencies:

> ... 180,000 happy Stockholmers in royal revelry ... How beautiful she is, cheered the people ... The bridal couple in radiant cortège. Blue-and-yellow flags. Happy onlookers in quadruple lines. Salutes and cheers for the royal sloop ...Here is my Silvia – your queen ... 'Welcome to us' ... The day we got a queen. SILVIA'S FAIRY-TALE WEDDING ... Joyful family ceremony in front of millions. 200 years since the last time ... The picture TV couldn't show: The kiss Sweden has awaited for four years ... Not one colour-TV left for hire for the wedding tomorrow ... Perfect TV-wedding for millions. 180,000 BY THE CORTÈGE ...[13]

This is obviously not just any royal wedding. The huge media attention is legitimized by a news value bluntly expressed in numbers: "'YES' – AND THERE WAS A QUEEN. 500 million witnesses to the wedding on TV".[14] Following this logic, 500 million people cannot possibly be wrong; this is indeed a truly important event, made public all over the globe by international news media. The great number of television viewers worldwide legitimates the enormous media coverage, which in turn has rendered possible the huge public attendance of the wedding through the media, in a perfect circular definition.

In fact, the presence of the masses is of great importance for the successful execution of this ceremonial occasion. Sweden in the 1970s was in many ways a class society with clearly articulated divides between the political right and left. The strong Social Democratic Party had taken the initiative to a revision of the constitution, passed in 1974 and depriving the Swedish monarch of political power, leaving him a symbolic position only. In this context of potential conflicts and disagreements regarding the present as well as the future role of the Bernadotte family, the king's wedding provided an excellent opportunity to re-establish the centrality of monarchy in the minds of the Swedish people. This appeal to the popular appetite for festivities is indeed evident in the organization and invention of easily accessible public features during the wedding day – a long cortège in an open carriage around central Stockholm, a romantic boat trip and a spectacular disembarkment by the Royal Castle, where all streets are cleared for thousands of onlookers – but also in the news media's eagerness to cooperate in the virtual gathering of the absent masses, thus optimizing their chances to watch the masses present at the scene. The masses are important as a symbol of royal power – there is no king without his subjects – and the more, the merrier. Or in this case, perhaps: the more, the mightier.

In conclusion: the media's participation in the royal wedding in 1976 is neither status rising, as in 1888, nor challenging, as in 1932 – it is simply represented as a normal and necessary element of contemporary society. Arguably, the myth of the mediated centre is completely naturalized by this time, and as a consequence it is also made invisible. The media make a point of complementing each other; what is not seen on TV is shown in the press, and the other way around, in the tailor-made model of the mediated social centre. The wedding reports from Stockholm in 1976 surely sketch the contours of a media event, coronation style[15] – except that the actual king of the day is not the newlywed Carl Gustaf, but the news media themselves.

Beyond the Myth

These analyses have demonstrated that the myth of the mediated centre is a journalistic construction, with a present, a past and an origin in time. The present material, however, does not allow us to say exactly when this myth was naturalized. Neither does it allow us to draw conclusions about the state of the idea of the mediated centre today. Still, the study does accomplish something important in deconstructing the myth of the mediated centre and foregrounding its processual character, as well as acknowledging the crucial role of different journalistic genres and modes of representation in the gradual establishment of this myth.

Arguably, the chronology preceding the seemingly perfect transparency of the naturalized myth of the mediated centre also demonstrates a significant shift in importance between the actors in the social centre and its mediators. As this tale of three royal weddings reveals, the focus of journalistic interest has widened from concentrated observations of the royal couples to a self-conscious foregrounding of the media's necessary presence in the very centre of attention. In fact, one could say that the concept as such takes on a meta-dimension when the news media themselves are placed in the middle of the mediated centre.

Nick Couldry stresses the close connections between media events and the construction of an idea or a sense of 'the centre', something the present study confirms and also displays in visual and verbal detail.[16] In a later article, he sketches a possible itinerary for media studies beyond the media-centrism implied and promoted by the myth of the mediated centre.[17] This route leads out of the national centres and into the periphery of local, subcultural and alternative media. However, I wish to propose yet another road in order to deconstruct and get beyond the mediated centre. This is the path of historical media studies, a direction I have briefly explored here. Studying the past is an eminent way to get new perspectives on the present and thereby be able to understand the present in a different way. The myth of the mediated centre is undoubtedly central to contemporary journalism (and to media studies), but it has not always existed, and will not continue to exist forever. A final *caveat* should be added, though: Studying the past does not mean focusing entirely on change and ignoring continuity. Media studies are to a considerable extent oriented towards change, failing to see the things that remain the same, or that change very slowly. While we intently watch (the myth of) the mediated centre gradually change into the media-centred society, it is important not to overlook the archaic myth of royalty, whose immovable perseverance and continuing public influence earns its place in the centre of attention.

Notes

1. See for example the annual World Press Freedom Index published by Reporters without borders/Reporters sans frontières (RSF), available on www.rsf.org (11 August 2008).
2. Jürgen Habermas, *The Structural Transformation of the Public Sphere* (1962; Cambridge: Polity Press, 1989).
3. Nick Couldry, *Media Rituals: A Critical Approach* (London: Routledge, 2003), p. 46.
4. "Prins Oscar", *Svenska Dagbladet* 16 March 1888; "Prins Oscars blifvande ställning", *Afton-bladet* 17 March 1888; "Prins Oscars samhällsställning", *Dagens Nyheter* 19 March 1888.
5. A collage technique without specific references is applied in order to create condensed versions of prominent discursive themes in the wedding reports. All quotations are from the papers and the period indicated in the overview of the material.
6. "Förmälningen", *Aftonbladet* 15 March 1888 and "Fröken Ebba Munck", *Idun* 30 January 1888, p. 30.
7. Ibid.
8. *Idun* 23 March 1888.

9. Compare Michael Schudson, *Discovering the News: A Social History of American Newspapers* (New York: Basic Books, 1978); John Hartley, *Popular Reality: Journalism, Modernity, Popular Culture* (London: Arnold, 1996).
10. "Bröllopet i Bournemouth", *Aftonbladet* 23 March 1888; "Bröllopet i Bournemouth", *Svenska Dagbladet* 23 March 1888.
11. Eveo [Erik Wilhelm Olson], "GUSTAF ADOLF TACKAR PÅ 30 METER LJUDFILM", *Svenska Dagbladet* 20 October 1932.
12. Åbergsson, "Prinsen framför sitt tack genom SF-Tobis", *Dagens Nyheter* 20 October 1932.
13. The collage technique used earlier reappears here.
14. *Aftonbladet* 19 June 1976, news bill.
15. Daniel Dayan & Elihu Katz, *Media Events: The Live Broadcasting of History* (Cambridge, Mass.: Harvard University Press, 1992).
16. Couldry, *Media Rituals*, p. 66.
17. Nick Couldry, "Transvaluing Media Studies: Or, Beyond the Myth of the Mediated Centre", in James Curran & David Morley (eds), *Media and Cultural Theory* (London: Routledge, 2006), pp. 177-194.

Long Live the King! Long Live the Press!
The Monarchy and the Legitimacy of the Press

Patrik Lundell

In his book *Queen Victoria: First Media Monarch*, John Plunkett writes: "Victoria's media making was as much about the media's making of its own mythology."[1] In contrast to Plunkett, it is precisely that aspect which interests me; the duality is of course there, but I focus not on the monarchy's but on the medium's mediation and strivings for legitimacy. My example is not Queen Victoria but King Oscar II, more precisely in the context of the international press congress in Stockholm in 1897. And the media institution in focus is the newspaper press.[2]

The press congress in Stockholm was the fourth international congress to be arranged, and it attracted approximately 400 journalists from around the world, the lion's share of them being Europeans, and men – only five delegates were women.[3] Host and organizer was the Swedish Press Club. The congress lasted for four days, and the programme contained, besides the internal negotiations, visits to museums, cathedrals and the Opera, dinners and parties, steamship journeys and a swimming gala. Of course, the visiting journalists were also guided through the great exhibition area, because the press congress – and this certainly was not by chance – coincided with the Stockholm Exhibition of 1897. The exhibition, in its turn, overlapped – and neither was this a coincidence – the king's 25-year jubilee as monarch.[4]

An important point made here is that manifestations of this kind – and their reception by various audiences – can be seen both as a measure of and as a means for attaining status and legitimacy. In other words, the manifestations, including their audiences, also function as media. In addition, such manifestations are always the result of a co-production, involving various interested parties. In the case discussed, the press and its power and importance for the Swedish nation were central messages.[5] One important agent, spectator and medium was the king.

The Media History of the Press

Conditions are compelling. Any exercise of power requires the production of meaning that conveys and confirms the legitimacy of that power. Power must take a form before it can be conceived and understood; it must be symbolized before it can be acknowledged and respected.[6] How has the press communicated its power through language, rites and symbols? How has it created its strong trademark? And what role can the monarchy be said to have played in these processes? Before analysing the congress of 1897, I will offer some preliminary methodological remarks on these questions.[7] A public event like the press congress naturally responds to several ambitions. One prominent and more or less pronounced aim was to improve the status of the Swedish press, both internationally and at home. Other, more modest or quite different media forms – like statues, medallions, history books, press house architecture, posters, stamps, memoirs, novels, films et cetera – can also be considered when these issues are studied historically. Such expressions are an obvious part of what the press or journalists *do*, as obvious as the production of newspaper texts and illustrations. They can, in other words, be seen as a form of journalistic endeavours, or put perhaps more provocatively as a form of journalism. Newspapers are but one of the forms in which the press has manifested itself. The media history of the press is a far wider field than the mere study of newspapers.

The question of which medium played the most important role – for example the newspaper or the congress (of which the latter consisted of numerous other media, one of them being the king) – is only meaningful if it is specified quite narrowly. However, assuming *a priori* that other media are secondary to newsprint is tantamount to adopting the self-image of the press, that is, to adopting and confirming notions that the perspective argued for here wants to historicize. Of course, the different media forms involved mutually amplify or at least impinge on each other, and naturally the newspapers play a crucial role in these processes. This, however, does not change the fact that kings, too, can function, and have functioned, historically as media.

These phenomena – the doings and writings of different agents – must not be reduced to a strategic power game. Mutual benefits and common interests, rather than competition, are the leitmotif. That external actors share the values of the press is partly the result of these values having been staged in various media – this is the starting point for the perspective argued for here. The press congress of 1897 mattered; it played a formative role. The press has successfully created a strong trademark, not only among the general public (and its own practitioners), but also among artists, scholars, politicians, industrialists and kings. However, straightforward linear models of diffusion poorly describe the far more complex interaction. It is rather a question of a legitimating circle. Furthermore, boundaries are porous. The politician can also be (and very often has been) an editor; the best friend of the editor is perhaps a historian; the industrialist shares economic interests with the publisher (who, for that matter, *is* an industrialist); the monarch and the editor share fundamental ideological assumptions. Such overlapping is common, and social networks undoubtedly play a crucial role.

Internal tensions and external actors influence the mediated self-image. This can be understood in terms of negotiations with resulting compromises, be studied from the perspective of a Bourdieuan struggle for capital and the establishing and maintenance of a specific field, or be interpreted in terms of Gramscian notions of hegemony. This applies not only to the elites, but also to the larger audience, representing the so-called general public. Actual audiences do not swallow just anything – certainly not when they are expected to play an active part (for example as cheering crowds). If the staged self-image is to be accepted, it must always touch the chords of society's predominant values.

Rather than describing the efforts to attain legitimacy as images that are 'spread' through *one* channel (newspapers) by *one* actor (the media institution called the press), they should be seen as a mutual exchange between various media and various actors. Different audiences have been resources for the press, just as the press has been a resource for them. Instead of treating proper journalism, the spreading of the self-image, and the receptions of different audiences (from the man on the street to members of the royal family) as clearly defined and separate areas, they must be seen as constituting and thus legitimizing each other.[8]

The values staged are often experienced, by the press and others, not as values, but as natural features of the medium. Cold-blooded calculations and deliberate delusions are only a marginal part of the phenomenon. This is primarily a question of an inherent logic, of efforts indissolubly attached to influence, power and economics at one level, and professional identity at another. By necessity, this logic cannot operate independently of the audiences and media it engages. The relatively scarce elements of hard-core propaganda, however, do not make the study of these phenomena less important.

The King of the Press Congress

One newspaper claimed that Oscar II's popularity in the whole civilized world, combined with his jubilee, constituted one of the most important reasons for making Stockholm host of the fourth press congress.[9] In reality, a diplomatic game had been necessary, in which the king himself took an active part. He had promised a dinner for the congress at the royal palace at Drottningholm, outside Stockholm, and he had assured that this honour was not to be bestowed on any of the other congresses coinciding with the great exhibition. These promises were not official.[10] On the other hand, His Majesty's grant of 10,000 kronor to the congress was common knowledge.[11]

Already on their arrival to Sweden, a large group of journalists paid their respect to the Swedish monarch in form of a telegram. This set the tone. His entrance into the House of the Nobility, the location for the opening of the congress, was received with loud cheers, and the president of the congress, Austrian Wilhelm Singer, proclaimed a "Long live the King!". King Oscar gave a short speech, which once again unleashed what the newspapers called an "ear-splitting storm of acclamations and shouts".[12] In company with the crown prince, the king also attended the gala performance at the Opera. And during his speech at the dinner at Drottningholm – a dinner commonly acknowledged as the climax of the congress – he was continually interrupted by applause and cheers from the thus assembled international press corps. And once again president Singer proclaimed: "Long live the King!" More could be noted. At the so-called Press Pavilion in the Exhibition area, for instance, there was a large portrait of the king, donated by a private entrepreneur, and, as the congress was over, a deputation from the Press Club called on the king and conveyed the thankfulness of the Swedish press. All this was of course extensively covered in the newspapers, internationally as well as at home.

The press congress was made possible, supported and given shape by various interested parties, one of whom was the Swedish king. And the congress no doubt functioned as a means of marketing the Swedish monarchy and the person Oscar II (besides, of course, Swedish culture, tourism, trade and industry). This publicity had openly been used as an argument for investing in the congress. The utility, thus, was mutual.

Kungliga paviljongen och Pressens paviljong.

With common interests. "The Royal Pavilion and the Press Pavilion". *Göteborgs Handels-och Sjöfarts-Tidning* 26 June 1897.

Naturally, these songs of praise can be seen as sheer fawning and fulsome flattery, with the prospect of being rewarded. To end the analysis at this point, however, would be a simplification. There was a very great community of interests. The Swedish press perceived furthering Swedish trade and industry, as well as culture and tourism, as an obvious task, not least in the peaceful competition between nations of the civilized world. This self-image as a national force and co-power also included, as a rule, a supportive role in relation to the monarchy. One of the visiting journalists, in one of the hundreds of speeches delivered, spoke of the "patriotic firmness" of the Swedish press, a firmness that so impeccably united "the principles of civic freedom with true Teutonic fidelity to the Royal House".[13]

However, this does not mean that we have to yield to an evolutionary historiography, looking at the ideals of the press as immature, and saying that the press had not yet come very far in its development and therefore could hardly have conducted itself in a different way. That would mean simplifying coarsely and adopting a most narrow perspective. Firstly, there actually did exist a critical discussion within the press, and secondly, the press also presented itself as a far from humble co-power.

In internal debates at the Press Club prior to the great Exhibition, the critical mission of the press was discussed. Everyone admitted that they faced a problem, and in principle everyone agreed on the critical mission of the press.[14] After the event, it is easy to say that these declarations came to nought. Collectively, the Swedish press was more or less a marketing channel for the Exhibition. An illustrative example is offered by Hjalmar Branting (who later became Swedish Prime Minister) and his newspaper *Social-Demokraten*. Branting was one of the most fervent advocates of critical journalism in the Press Club debates. He wished the foreign pressmen welcome, but he hoped that the hospitality would not conceal all the social evils of Swedish society; he hoped, as he put it in his paper, that they would not come as "publicity makers".[15] During the beginning of the congress, *Social-Demokraten* often contained sceptical remarks on the press's cheers for the king and sarcastic comments on official reverences paid to the press.[16] However, Branting had also managed to ward off a major strike, planned to coincide with the opening of the exhibition.[17] And as the congress proceeded, the softer *Social-Demokraten* became. Oscar II's speech at Drottningholm was said to be the best the king had ever delivered, and on the return journey from the dinner party, the paper noted a flaming royal monogram – "exceedingly strikingly arranged".[18] The exhibition has been analysed as a sort of pacifying seduction for the otherwise threatening masses; partly the same can be said about the congress and the press, even an angry Social Democrat was seduced.[19]

The Interpretations of the Press

Nonetheless, Hjalmar Branting as well as the rest of the Swedish press corps obviously celebrated ideals different from those manifested in practice. These ideals have very often, before as well as after, been acknowledged as essential to the press, yes, almost as specific to the medium itself. The discrepancies between ideals and practice become even more evident if we study the way in which the press described itself in the official rhetoric. Undoubtedly the most frequent metaphor was "the forth estate", which in Swedish, since it was established in 1830s, has been expressed as "the third power of the State", the other two being the Parliament and the government, the latter symbolically represented by the king. One often spoke of the enormous power of the press when it came to moulding public opinion.

This self-depiction, in its turn, can be compared with what different actors in fact acknowledged the press to be. Financial support and dinner parties were of course a kind of recognition. But what, for example, did the king actually say? In his speech at Drottningholm he was obviously positive, not to say flattering. However, he also expressed reservations and conditions: "as long as" the press assumed its "proper responsibility" it would be held as "a great blessing"; its freedom in Sweden, the monarch went on, was almost unlimited – and this was because the press had always understood how to "unite the respect for lawfulness and loyalty" with "the ancient Swedish love for freedom and independence".[20] Importantly, the vocabulary of the king was quite different from that of the press. He most certainly did not call the press "the third power of the State"; he actually did not refer to the press in any terms of *power*.

Symbolic acknowledgements no doubt took place. These, however, must be given apt proportions. They should furthermore be compared to how the press used them, how the press interpreted them and gave them meaning. For instance, the fact that the king was present at the opening of the congress was front-page news. The event was called "the recognition by the Crown"; by comparison with the newspapers' celebration of the monarch, this was "a far more important and fundamental acknowledgement of the power that the press now represents in our society". Something "significant and symbolic" had been witnessed.[21]

Reports from the international press started to flow into Swedish newspaper columns. The Danish *Politiken* claimed that Oscar II "had made a clean cut with old prejudice and that he had treated the press as a great power"; *Echo de Paris* wrote that the Swedish monarch had "glorified" the press; *Vossiche Zeitung* told of "an enlightened and truly modern sovereign" who understood "the power and importance" of the press. "It was a triumph", exclaimed *Gazette de Lausanne*: "On its journey through Europe, the fourth estate has been greeted as an equal to kings and emperors. A sign of the times! Thirty years ago none of this was possible."[22]

Interpreting the king's treatment of the press *as* a kind of recognition is not the same as when actors at the time claimed that it *actually was* one. The newspaper-reading public could read for themselves that the king had acknowledged the press as a great power; the papers said that he had glorified the press. And if the congress was called a symbolic and significant event then – in a sense – it actually *was* one; the statement was self-fulfilling – who else would take care of the news evaluation?

However, the public did not only learn about the congress through the newspaper columns. The congress in itself was a highly public affair – the

The king acknowledges the press – that was how the press interpreted the solemn opening of the press congress. *Pressen* 1898 (2).

press literally put itself on display, in the streets and parks of Stockholm and on steamboat excursions. The king had a ringside seat, from which place he also heard the cheers of the people (cheers in honour of both himself and the press); these cheers reached him directly and through the newspapers; and this cheering – *nota bene!* – was partly the result of the king actually being there. In this sense, it is obvious that the monarch, through his physical person, mediated the messages of the congress. Thus, the congress attained status because of its highly esteemed audience – both in a social (the royal family) and in a professional sense (highly respected international journalists). But the popular enthusiasm and the sheer number of people gathered around the undertakings of the congress – almost as representatives of the Swedish people as a whole – also served a similar purpose.

The consensus was striking. Critical remarks certainly stood out as exceptions and rather served to accentuate the mutual understanding. Two of these exceptions can be noted, one from the left and one from the right. The Socialist Axel Danielsson in his paper *Arbetet* in Malmö wrote with distaste of "the intimate mix with the royal family". The foreigners should not be blamed, according to Danielsson, but the Swedish journalists ought to be ashamed of themselves. According to Danielsson, the message in the king's speech at Drottningholm – which even Branting's *Social-Demokraten* had been seduced by – was spelled: obedience and loyalty. Had the Stockholm editors listened at all? Nothing but a great lie had been staged: "The foreign journalists have seen a Sweden which does not exist, a wonderful nation with a liberal king, an amiable upper class, which warmly cherish the men of free speech, and a people who pass their lives by the bottle of Swedish arrack in total bliss."[23]

From the notorious conservative editor Alfred Hedenstierna in *Smålands-Posten* came diametrically opposed objections. The visiting journalists by no means constituted an honourable and respectable community, but they were rather a lot of riff-raff; if anyone had been fooled and compromised, it was unfortunately the Swedish king when he fed them at Drottningholm.[24]

Concluding Remarks

The present article's focus on a public event must not be understood as implying that such events necessarily play a more important role in our understanding of the history of the legitimacy of the press than do other kinds of mediations. It is well worth focusing on low-key productions of meaning. Moreover, this specific event should not be seen, firstly, as a historical milestone of particular significance. However, it can be argued that there are methodological advantages, besides those case studies generally offer, in terms of depth and concreteness. The events distinctly reveal mechanisms and overlapping media practices that are always at hand. They open our eyes to more general aspects of questions about legitimacy and self-image. The notion that actual journalism, the spreading of its ideals, and the reception of the audiences always constitute each other becomes exceptionally clear: In some respects the elements of straightforward propaganda are obvious – at the same time as the dependence of other actors is evident. And no definite line can be drawn between where these events end and where the newspaper reports begin.

Furthermore, the nebular Press takes on a manageable form in various organizations, committees or groups composed of specific actors. The catchword level, which predominates, offers in all its superficiality notions in concentrated form, a sort of fixed ideal perpetuated in texts, images and gestures. At the same time, a condition of the strength of these manifestations is their conceptual vagueness. Concepts like 'power', 'freedom', 'independence' and 'responsibility' are open enough to unite political opponents. This does not mean, however, that the picture is one-dimensional or unambiguous. There are always tensions, and the manifest expression is always the product of negotiations and compromises, which can also be revealed from letters, minutes and other archive material. Thus, it becomes possible to identify the common interests, as well as which actors have been dominant, and over whom.

The turn of the century 1900 was a formative period for both the monarchy and the newspaper press. Of course, the Stockholm Exhibition of 1897, combined with the jubilee of the monarch, was a very specific and unique occasion. National values and prestige were at stake, and therefore one could argue that prevalent journalistic rules were set aside. Add to that a substantial flow of alcohol. When the party was over, the press once again opened its critical eye, now from a strengthened position. Surely, there was such an effect, but hardly any such conscious strategy. Several factors make such an interpretation unlikely. Firstly, there is the conspicuous mutuality and the obvious common interests. Secondly, such an analysis would be extremely reductionistic and ahistorical: The press is made a critical examiner and the Crown a conservative brake block – no more, no less. And thirdly, it could be argued that unique events (an exhibition, the Olympics, a world war, the funeral of a princess) just as well amplify and make visible what is there all the time. And besides, one could always ask: When have history's periods of normality actually taken place? Moreover, the historiography staged during the congress was repeated on several occasions afterwards. When Oscar II died in 1907, he was hailed for his significance for the congress and for the free press on the whole.[25] In 1924, the Press Club published a chronicle of its endeavours and the same narrative was repeated.[26] Oscar II's role in and for this narrative of the press's path towards legitimacy and status has since been reduced considerably. Nowadays, the relation is described almost entirely in terms of struggle and oppression. Such a historiography is utterly incomplete, not to say fundamentally untrue.

Even in retrospect, it is reasonable to see the congress of 1897 as a symbolic turning point – my point, however, is that this is highly dependent on the fact that it was *made* a symbol through various media and with the aid of different audiences. One very important actor, who played his role both as medium and spectator, was the Swedish king, Oscar II.

Notes

1. John Plunkett, *Queen Victoria: First Media Monarch* (Oxford: Oxford University Press, 2003), p. 7.
2. The article develops a perspective in Patrik Lundell's "Pressen är budskapet: Journalistkongressen och den svenska pressens legitimitetssträvanden", in Anders Ekström, Solveig Jülich & Pelle Snickars (eds), *1897: Mediehistorier kring Stockholmsutställningen* (Stockholm: SLBA, 2006).
3. No specific references will be given to basic facts on the congress; they are easily found in the excessive reports of any of the Stockholm newspapers at the time. Many of the quotations can be found in a number of these papers; to make it easy for the interested reader, I have in those cases used one paper, *Dagens Nyheter*.
4. On the exhibition, see Anders Ekström, *Den utställda världen: Stockholmsutställningen 1897 och 1800-talets världsutställningar* (Stockholm: Nordiska museets förlag, 1994). Various media-historical perspectives on the exhibition are given in Ekström, Jülich & Snickars (eds).
5. The event was highly engaged in the construction of what Nick Couldry, *Media Rituals: A Critical Approach* (London/New York: Routledge, 2003), passim, terms "the myth of the mediated centre", a perspective developed in this book by Kristina Widestedt.
6. See for example Michael Walzer, "On the Role of Symbolism in Political Thought", *Political Science Quarterly* 1967 (82), p. 194; and Lynn Hunt, *Politics, Culture, and Class in the French Revolution* (Berkeley: University of California Press, 1986), p. 54. See also Mary Douglas, *How Institutions Think* (London: Routledge & Kegan Paul, 1987), p. 45.
7. For a more elaborated introduction to these perspectives, see Patrik Lundell, "The Medium is the Message: The Media History of the Press", *Media History* 2008 (1).
8. Compare John Hartley, *Popular Reality: Journalism, Modernity, Popular Culture* (London: Arnold, 1996), on "the mediasphere" and the view that journalism *is* "meanings" and "readership".
9. "Den fjärde internationella journalistkongressen", *Nya Dagligt Allehanda* 23 June 1897.
10. Riksarkivet (The National Archives), 77 Sveriges Pressarkiv, Publicistklubbens arkiv, Protokoll vid årsmöten och klubbsammanträden, A1A:8, Sammanträdet den 11 sept. 1896, §7.

11. 10,000 kronor in 1897 equals approximately 60,000 euro (based on retailer price index) or 680,000 euro (based on salary index for industrial labour) in 2008.
12. "Journalistkongressen"/"Det högtidliga öppnandet", *Dagens Nyheter* 26 June 1897.
13. Dr. Lauser quoted in "Middagen på Hasselbacken", *Dagens Nyheter* 28 June 1897.
14. Riksarkivet, 77 Sveriges Pressarkiv, Publicistklubbens arkiv, Protokoll vid årsmöten och klubbsammanträden, A1A:8, Sammanträdet den 20 nov. 1896, §4.
15. Hj[almar] B[rantin]g, "Världspressens möte", *Social-Demokraten* 25 June 1897.
16. See for example "Journalistkongressen", *Social-Demokraten* 26 June 1897.
17. Ekström, p. 117.
18. "Drottningholmsfesten", *Social-Demokraten* 26 June 1897.
19. On "the *conciliatory* element of exhibition history", see Ekström, p. 236.
20. Oscar II quoted in "Festen å Drottningholm", *Dagens Nyheter* 29 June 1897.
21. "Den första statsmakten och den tredje", *Dagens Nyheter* 26 June 1897.
22. The foreign papers quoted in (the recurring headline) "Journalistkongressen inför utlandet", *Dagens Nyheter* 1, 9, 10 and 6 July 1897.
23. Signature Didrik, "Brandsyn", *Arbetet* 5 July 1897.
24. Signature Sigurd [Alfred Hedenstierna], "Dagskrönika", *Smålands-Posten* 8 July 1897; this article can be said to anticipate a famous attack on the Swedish press by the author and later Nobel Prize winner Verner von Heidenstam in his "Våra tidningar", *Svenska Dagbladet* 23 October 1897.
25. See for example signature Partout, "Oscar II och pressen", *Svenska Dagbladet* 16 December 1907.
26. Valfrid Spångberg, "Publicistklubben 1874-1924", in *Publicistklubben* (Stockholm: Publicistklubbens förlag, 1924).

An Enduring History Lesson

National Honour and Hegemonic Masculinity in the Early Swedish Blockbuster Karl XII

Tommy Gustafsson

Between 1892 and 1914, Sweden carried out several significant rearmaments, strengthening Sweden's armed forces to the same degree as most other European countries. During the First World War, however, the Swedish defence soon became hopelessly outdated in comparison with the nations fighting on the continent. Furthermore, throughout the war, Sweden was shaken by severe inner disturbances: hunger strikes caused by badly planned rationings and outright mutinies within the armed forces. This sped up the process of democracy, giving all Swedish males the right to vote and thus a parliamentary government in 1917. The political party that gained the most from these changes was the Social Democratic Party – by tradition and principle against the military. In light of the facts that Europe was fed up with war, that Russia was broken, and that Sweden had become a member of the League of Nations, the Social Democrats, in collaboration with the Liberal Party, wanted to cut the armed forces budget drastically.[1]

At the same time, the right-wing parties and the military leadership, who had been the orchestrators of the great rearmaments before the war, claimed that the threat from Russia, now in the guise of the Soviet Union, must not be underestimated. In 1919, a parliamentary investigation of the future of the armed forces was initiated, and this was followed by a heated debate that lasted for six years. In 1925, opponents of the military were victorious, and the decision was taken that Sweden, in one swift stroke, was to cut its armed forces budget by no less than 50 per cent.[2]

In September 1922, in the midst of the fierce debate, rumours of a film production on the subject of King Charles XII started to circulate. Several Swedish military officers were named as the instigators of what was perceived as a blunt propaganda film to strengthen public sympathy for the armed forces. A company, AB Historisk Film, was founded with a rear admiral, a lieutenant-colonel and a captain on the board of directors, and financially backed by the fourth board member, the wealthy engineer Herman Rasch. After several problematical detours, including the start of a failed film production in Germany, the shooting of the first part of *Karl XII* finally began in March 1924.[3]

The practice of using old Swedish war kings as symbols of national romanticism was nothing new. Charles XII had earlier been used as a symbol by the temperance movement, and the raising of a statue of Charles XII had caused riots in Stockholm in 1868. However, Charles XII really came into prominence with the release of Verner von Heidenstam's novel, *The Carolines*, in 1897.[4] This was the start of the creation of an infatuated cult around Charles XII and Sweden's period as a major European power that the political right could exploit to gain public support for its purposes.[5] The use of Charles XII and other Swedish war kings had always been contested by the left-wing parties as an example of dangerous nationalism and a romanticization of war, but by holding the hegemonic position in Swedish political life, the political right could describe the left's anti-militarism as an unpatriotic standpoint and uphold support for the rearmaments until 1914.[6]

Sweden is not known for its war films. *Karl XII* (1925, John W. Brunius) – a film that in two parts chronologically follows the life and actions of Swedish eighteenth century war king, Charles XII (†1718) – is one of a very few thoroughly executed Swedish war films with restaged gigantic battle scenes.[7] In the 1920s, a few big budget historical films like *Karl XII* were produced that included some war scenery. In the 1930s and during the Second World War, around fifteen home defence propaganda films were made, but these films did not include the actual display of violence and were, furthermore, mostly produced as comedies.[8]

Moreover, the two parts of *Karl XII* had the impressive running time of five hours and twelve minutes (or 6.145 meters), and it was the most expensive Swedish production to date with huge scenes that included tens of thousands of extras, uniforms, horses, et cetera, and that were shot on location in several historic sites all around Sweden and Europe. With admissions that reached the one million mark – at a time when Sweden's population amounted to six million – *Karl XII* became a formidable audience success. In addition to this, the film was exported to nineteen countries: the UK, the US, Germany, India, Japan, and Argentina, to name a few. In spite of these accomplishments, *Karl XII* turned out to be an overwhelming economic disaster owing to its gigantic production budget.[9] Although the original intention to arouse patriotic feelings that would prevent the downsizing of the armed forces failed in the end, the film nevertheless represents a unique case in point as a vehicle for the display of both masculinity and history. Here, I am going to concentrate on the exploitation of Charles XII as an ambiguous symbol of an idealized, hegemonic masculinity. But first, I will explore the fact that, despite huge differences in opinion about the political intention, the film itself did evoke a strong feeling of national honour that at the time was closely connected to masculinity.

National Honour

"Karl XII" is well worth becoming the Swedish national film above all others, both for the subject's patriotic and heroic characterization, and for the production's vigour and dignity.[10]

Sweden now has a national work of film art that will last; one which is pretty remarkable in the young history of the film medium. [...] and not without satisfaction one is able to point out the fact that this film, from the first frame to the last, is Swedish – something which holds the promise of a bright future for Swedish film. Because it really does have a splendid future, that is, when certain circumstances in Europe have been regulated so that the European and thereby the Swedish film can once again obtain some elbowroom in the overwhelming competition with America.[11]

These quotes are taken from reviews in two conservative newspapers. Hence, it is no surprise that the reviewers are proud of the completion of the new film, and eagerly call attention to the patriotic theme and the Swedish production. A left-wing paper, on the other hand, began its review with these words: "Charles XII is, to be sure, the Grand-Swedish patriotism's national saint. This king has, especially among highly positioned military officers, been the subject of an almost mentally deranged cult".[12] Nevertheless, after having totally condemned the film for its subject, King Charles XII, and for the bombastic and neo-nationalistic production, the reviewer still writes: "However, if one overlooks the fancifully shaped story and just considers the film as a film, then it must be said that it is truly a magnificent work of film art, probably the most magnificent ever brought forth in Sweden".[13]

In the 1910s and the beginning of the 1920s, this small nation in the northern periphery of Europe could pride itself in its successful film export. This period, mythologically coined the Golden Age in Swedish film history, had recently faded out when the two parts of *Karl XII* appeared.[14] This was in fact seen as the film that was supposed to resurrect Swedish film and reinstate it on the international film market after a few years in fallow. And regardless of the strongly differing political opinions about the warrior king himself, all reviews, from the far left to the far right, shared the same admiration for the gigantic grand-scale film production.

As the quotations from the reviews of *Karl XII* indicate, a mere film was able to grant its country a certain amount of national honour, at a time when film culture was generally looked down upon. Furthermore, this national honour was closely tied to masculinity, as the reviewers perceived the film to be a distinctly male enterprise. "Swedish film was", as one critic wrote, "after all, still capable of achieving great deeds – and of succeeding! There are thus still men with enough enthusiasm for film, willing to risk huge sums of money on 'arty' productions!"[15] In another review this notion is even more explicit: "the film's last part is characterized by a stern seriousness, a manly accentuated commitment which makes it marvellously captivating, not to say deeply moving. One is aware of the honest masculine grip of it all. This is Swedish men's artistic tribute to one of the greatest Swedish men who has ever lived".[16]

This can be connected to what Tallak Moland has called the construction of a specific Nordic masculinity in the first decades of the twentieth century, as the words "man", "manliness" and "manly" were used more explicitly to display masculine deeds and achievements. Others have interpreted this overt emphasis as a crisis for masculinity, but Moland sees this as a sign that marked the early twentieth century as a particularly prosperous time for male power.[17] On the other hand, Sweden had recently introduced a compulsory military service, which was ideologically motivated by the understanding that Swedish males, not having been to war for a hundred years, had become soft and thus lost a vital part of their manliness.[18] Throughout history, national honour has also been closely tied to war, and thereby to men and masculinity, as the countless armies that have faced each other have, with few exceptions, been made up of men.[19] *Karl XII*, with its ideal display of war and the army on a grand historical scale, thus had the potential to inspire reluctant Swedish males for conscription, according to what George L. Mosse called "The Myth of the War Experience" – a process whereby war is romanticized by the designs of war cemeteries and memorials to fallen soldiers, but also by seemingly trivial cultural artefacts such as toys and films.[20] So despite the fact that on a certain level *Karl XII* only preached to the already convinced concerning the economic fate of the armed forces, on another level the film still appealed to a wider audience, not least through the use of well-known images of war and history to create what right-wing papers described as "a grand patriotic work of art [that] arouses the love for one's country"; "[t]he film is a splendid cultural historical representation with immense patriotic atmosphere".[21] In this way, the overall approval of the production becomes intertwined with the overt display of masculinity, regardless of differentiated political attitudes towards the film's original and failed intent.

Hegemonic Masculinity

Sweden has a long history of war. From the sixteenth century and up until 1814, Sweden more or less constantly waged war on its neighbouring countries: Russia, Poland, Denmark, the German states, and Norway. However, since 1814, Sweden has enjoyed a lasting peace that was not even disturbed by the two world wars. Since at least the nineteenth century, though, these old and often celebrated memories of war did have an immense influence on the writing of history and, consequently, constituted an important part of the Swedish historical consciousness and political life by the time the film *Karl XII* arrived on the scene.

In their propaganda, the political right frequently exploited Russia as a menace. A film about Charles XII made a perfect historical analogy, as Russia embodied the greatest threat to Sweden in the eighteenth century. However, a film about Charles XII did present the filmmakers with a historic conundrum: Tsar Peter the Great did, in the end, triumph over Charles XII on the battle-field of Poltava in 1709. Furthermore, the highly contested figure of Charles XII had to be depicted – not least for economic reasons – in a balanced way that did not alienate the audience altogether on either a historical or a politi-cal level. How did the filmmakers solve these apparent contradictions? Here it becomes relevant to pose questions about the construction, and positioning, of an exceedingly idealized hegemonic masculinity. According to R.W. Con-nell, hegemonic masculinity constitutes the type of masculinity that is currently accepted as the dominant one in a given society. Hegemonic masculinity is, consequently, not a fixed character type. "It is, rather, the masculinity that oc-cupies the hegemonic position in a given pattern of gender relations, a position always contestable".[22]

A fact that complicated matters further is that the film producers had chosen Gösta Ekman – again for economic reasons – to play the part of Charles XII. Ekman was a highly popular film and stage actor in Sweden at the time. How-ever, prior to *Karl XII*, he had mostly acted in comedies, and more seldom in serious dramas, where he was often celebrated for his good looks rather than for his acting skills. The year before he had played a stern Caroline soldier in the adventure film *The Currier of Charles XII*, only to be made a laughing stock by the entire body of film reviewers, who had severe reservations about Ekman's masculinity. His extravagant personality, which revealed a high degree of dandyism when it came to fashionable clothes and other accessories, clashed with their perception of how a manly Caroline should look and behave.[23] In Connell's theoretical structure of relational masculinities, Ekman's masculinity ought, accordingly, to be positioned at the absolute bottom, as a subordinate type of masculinity.[24] For him to take on the role of Charles XII – this "monstros-ity of braveness", as one reviewer wrote[25] – could thus present the filmmakers with some intricate problems, as this film was a vehicle for the promotion of male machismo *per se.*

As all mythological and yet historic figures, Charles XII was certainly sur-rounded by numerous and well-known legends – which often were spelled out as historical facts in the historiography of the time. The filmmakers worked with masculine contrasts in regard to these legends as a way to depict the competi-tion between the two combatants, Charles XII and Peter the Great (played by Russian actor Nicolai de Seversky). The film brings two of these legends into play: Charles XII's indifference to women and his absolutism, as he allegedly only drank water and never touched alcohol.

On only one occasion does the character of Charles XII show an interest in a woman – in a film that closely traces his life for five hours. This happens early on as he and his entourage, out on a hunting trip, visit a mansion in the countryside, where he meets the daughter of the house. After dinner, she ap-proaches the king with a towel and a bowl of water. When she is about to leave, the king stops her for a chat. The members of his entourage immediately notice

"A monstrosity of braveness". Gösta Ekman as Charles XII, the epitome of masculinity in Swedish historical consciousness in the 1920s. *Filmjournalen* 1925 (15-16).

that the king is being "gallant" and that this is something unusual. However, Charles XII displays his inexperience with women, as the only conversation he is able to make is about hunting.

Much more effort is put into demonstrating how the king avoids women. Most notable is his reaction to the seductive Aurora Königsmarck who, together with the king's adversary, King August of Poland, makes plans to lure Charles XII into an erotic trap with Aurora as the bait. When Charles XII finally meets her she is waiting for him in a carriage at the end of a bridge. At the sight of Aurora, the king becomes terribly frightened, turns his horse around and then sets off in full gallop into the horizon. Later on they meet again at a ball in Leipzig, which is organized in honour of Charles XII by the now defeated King August. When Aurora suddenly enters the room where the king resides, he desperately tries to leave but she stops him and asks: "Your majesty can't be afraid of me? Your Majesty, who knows the great art of always being victorious!" Charles XII appears angry, but cannot face her as he answers: "It isn't me who win the battles, countess! It is my soldiers who triumph! When I'm alone I'm quite helpless, as the countess must have noticed at the bridge!"

Peter the Great is portrayed in sharp contrast to Charles XII. He is married, but nonetheless gladly diverts himself with other women when the opportunity presents itself. During an ongoing campaign, the camera sneaks into the Tsar's tent and thus exposes a laughing and drinking Peter, being intimate with a young woman on his knee. Remarkable here is also Peter's conspicuous consumption of alcohol. He drinks heavily in all scenes in which he appears but two – generating the desired contrast to Charles XII, who only empties one glass of wine in the entire film to avoid being recognized as he travels incognito from Turkey to Sweden. The result of this, of course, is that Charles XII appears to be in control of his passions, while Peter the Great is depicted as a drunkard and womanizer without any self-control. The ability to master one's passions – sexual desires, alcohol, and the overt expression of emotions – also represented an important part of the masculine ideal at the time. A man who was unable to fight his passions risked being marked as a lesser man, even as unmanly.[26]

However, regarding the construction of masculinity, ideals and reality are not always compatible, as is shown by this indignant comment by one reviewer on the historical accuracy of the ball scene:

> Everything is genuine; whether it is scenes, costumes or milieu, and this apparently affects the audience, even if they do not have any previous knowledge of the historic events portrayed. From this viewpoint, there are some remarks to be made about the film. The big ball scene at the castle in Leipzig did not seem to be of the same quality as the rest. Here Charles XII was sullen and rude, characteristics that in reality were totally unknown to him. And it should be noticed that he was absolutely not as afraid of females as he was portrayed.[27]

Similar comments are also made about Charles XII's capacity to drink. When he drinks his only glass of wine so as not to be revealed, the reviewers described it as if Charles XII was, after all, able to "drink wine like a real man".[28] This in turn creates a paradox of masculinity, as the film leaves no doubt about the fact that Peter the Great could both drink and handle women like a real man – although the film intended to show the opposite. This is, in other words, a good example of how flexible the concept of hegemonic masculinity is, with a positioning that is always contestable or even interchangeable.

But Peter the Great is also portrayed as a hard working man who wants to haul Russia out of its oriental backwardness. Without rest he is making plans, both military and civic – such as building the new capital city, Saint Petersburg – all the while disciplining his lazy subjects with blows and threats. In one scene, Peter even cuts off the beard of a boyar when the boyar objects to moving the capital from Moscow.

This in many ways contradictory and positive contrast, that is, from a Swedish perspective, of Peter the Great actually becomes a necessity within the film

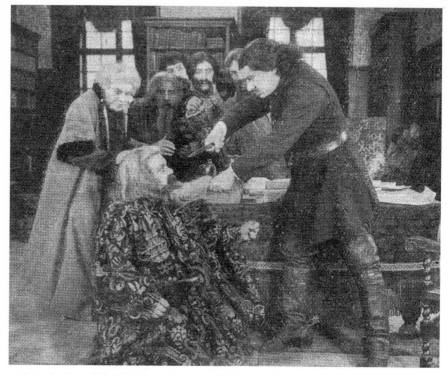

Peter the Great (Nicolai de Seversky) cuts of the beard of a boyar in *Karl XII*, thus displaying his lack of masculine self-control. *Filmnyheter* 1925 (20).

context. Otherwise, the drunken womanizer's final victory at Poltava would
have appeared to be even more humiliating for Sweden and the Swedish king.
Charles XII was, after all, defeated by a man of almost Western character and
not by an Eastern barbarian.

Military comradeship, or what Mosse describes as "the noblest expression of
[...] manliness"[29], is another idealized character trait that is strongly featured in
the film. Again this is used in a contrasting way, as the Swedish king eagerly
fraternizes with his soldiers, regardless of rank – and on several occasions even
takes personal care of their well-being – whereas the Russian tsar rules by repressive brutality and fear. The idealistic image of a Charles XII who fraternizes
with his soldiers supports the concept of the Myth of the War Experience, and
thereby romanticizes life in the modern compulsory Swedish army. This, in
fact, represents a skewed mirroring of the contemporary reality in the Swedish
armed forces, where the relationship between officers and private soldiers was
built on authoritarian cruelty rather than on mutual respect or comradeship.
According to this philosophy, the private and by this time conscripted Swedish
soldier was to be hardened through the use of constant violence and degrada-
tion – and to achieve complete obedience, the officers had absolute power, as
the privates could not make complaints.[30]

One last feature that separates the two combatants is their courage. Peter the Great is portrayed, as expected, as a calculating and deceitful coward who, for example, leaves his crumbling army behind in the face of defeat at the battle of Narva. Charles XII's courage, on the other hand, is portrayed as heroic, but also on the verge of being foolhardy. Time and again he exposes himself to unnecessary risks, for example when he sits on the edge of a trench while the bullets fly past him – a behaviour that eventually gets him killed (in the film and in reality). Another example is during the so-called Skirmish at Bender, where the king and a handful of soldiers fight against an Ottoman army. Charles XII is up front and refuses to retreat, despite the overwhelming superiority of the Ottomans. Finally, the Swedish soldiers are forced to wrestle him down and then drag him into safety.

This heroic yet thoughtless behaviour – typical for the genre of war films – was actually subjected to some criticism, mostly from left-wing papers that commentated ironically on this cinematic courage[31], while the right-wing papers more often than not greeted the same display of courage as something typically Swedish[32] – and thereby as a masculine quality, as the concepts of masculinity, the military and nation were interlaced.

Overall, *Karl XII*'s representations of Swedes and Russians are biased according to a standard mode of procedure, where the enemy is demonized and one's own side is glorified.[33] Even so, Gösta Ekman and Nicolai de Seversky were highly praised for their performances, in both left- and right-wing papers. Most of the reviews were also conscious of the film's contrasting division, but they chiefly focused on acting abilities rather than on historic accuracy or the contemporary significance that this acting entailed.[34] However, one Russian author, Vladimir Semitjoff, who lived in Stockholm, wrote an article after seeing the film in which he stands this contrast on its head. Semitjoff explains that he grew up with schoolbooks in which Peter the Great was the genius-man, the genius-soldier, the genius-scientist, schoolbooks that did not even mention the great Charles XII:

> Now I can see both Charles XII and Peter the Great on the screen in a grand film spectacle [...] and a strange metamorphosis takes place with my preconceptions [...] before me the mighty Tsar Peter is obscured and darkened, leaving room for another – hard as rock, cast in one piece – Charles XII. Peter does not exist on the screen. I see nothing but a ridiculous figure, a wimp, the first lover in a mediocre operetta, a braggart from a vaudeville, everything – but not a trace of the Tsar-genius or the Tsar-man, and even less of the Tsar-commander. [...] now it is the Swedes' turn to ask themselves where their hero-king's worthy opponent is and why the curious Russians have named their Peter – as he can be seen on the screen –"the Great". What greatness can be found in this neurotic?[35]

As this statement makes clear, the Swedish filmmakers succeeded in their effort to construct an ideal hegemonic masculinity by the use of sharp contrasts. But

Semitjoff's article also reveals the mobility of hegemonic masculinity, as it, according to Connell, constitutes a type of masculinity that is currently accepted as prevailing in a given society and not a fixed character type. From a Russian perspective, Charles XII and Peter the Great had simply switched positions with each other on the ladder of ideal, hegemonic masculinity.

Within the film context, Charles XII stands out as the personification of hegemonic masculinity in comparison to Peter the Great: the main distinction being that the Swedish king could control his passions, while the Russian tsar caved in to his and therefore appeared as more unmanly – at least according to notions of masculine ideals at the time. But as the analysis has shown, the set of ideals used in the film were not uncontested. Was the absolutism of Charles XII a sign of true manliness, or was it a manly deed to drink throughout the whole war and still win it, as Peter the Great did? And what about sex? In other words, the reality outside the film is always on the verge of breaking down the masculine ideals created within it. Nonetheless, within the film context, Charles XII is a more manly man than Peter the Great, but then how did the filmmakers solve the predicament of the historic fact that Peter eventually defeated Charles XII? After the battle of Poltava, the filmmakers simply erased Peter the Great out of the story, the result being that no further comparisons could be made, which in light of the devastating defeat would otherwise have risked the fragile hegemonic position of Charles XII's masculinity.

What perhaps could have been another threat to this creation of cinematic hegemonic masculinity was, of course, the fact that the role of Charles XII was played by the effeminate actor Gösta Ekman. However, by Ekman applying of a lifelike mask and acting in a more subdued manner, it seems as if the reviewers were able to forget his earlier, more light-hearted characters and his good looks. Very few of the reviewers made any remarks concerning his persona, but instead drowned him with praise: "Gösta Ekman's interpretation of the king is one of the most powerful individual performances that we ever have seen on the screen. He really does succeed in creating the character type most of us have when we think about Charles XII".[36] Apparently, Ekman created an image of Charles XII that corresponded very well with the one that existed in the Swedish historical consciousness of the 1920s, an image so powerful that it had the ability to palliate Ekman's earlier performances and his dandy masculinity.

An Enduring History Lesson

Karl XII sold one million tickets on its first theatrical run and, furthermore, was shortened and reedited with sound in 1933 for a second theatrical run – after which time the latter version circulated in the Swedish school system as a historically correct film lesson well into the 1980s.[37] The fact that the reedited version of *Karl XII* with added sound continued to be shown in the Swedish schools for almost 60 years is an example of how enduring history in itself can be. On the other hand, this constitutes the preservation of a moment in time, not of the actual past.

Robert Brent Toplin claims that cinematic history speaks, and even has to speak, to the present to make any sense to an audience, regardless of the historic event or person portrayed.[38] Mats Jönsson has even claimed that cinematic history tells us more about the period in which the film was produced and received than it does about the historic period depicted.[39] A feature film is also a perishable, in the sense that a commercial film is made to be consumed in the present and then shelved. Very few films, whether historical or not, have had a continued life after their first run.[40] But don't *Karl XII* and other examples of lasting cinematic history contradict this notion?

During these 60 years, the view of what history constituted and what subjects it was supposed to include changed radically. Within academia, the history of kings, wars and diplomacy gave way to histories with a more comprehensive focus on the everyday life of ordinary people.[41] The history of kings was, consequently, chiefly banished to popular books on history – which, needless to say, sustained a nineteenth century tradition of what history should be about.[42] Hence, during this time, *Karl XII*, at first a conventional element of what constituted history, is transformed to what is now perceived as a more popular universe of historical writing. At the same time, however, the vintage quality in itself turns the film into a seemingly truthful historical artefact, thus illustrating the importance of mediated history, because it is a fact that audiovisual media have been the dominant vehicle for conveying historical knowledge in the twentieth and twenty-first centuries. This phenomenon, what could be called postponed or delayed history, is of interest in its own right and deserves to be studied more methodically than has been done here.

Yet when it comes to the conserved, hegemonic masculinity of Gösta Ekman as Charles XII, one cannot help wondering to what length the perception of the dated acting style and heavy masking must have changed in Swedish classrooms. I find it hard to believe that pupils several decades later still perceived Ekman as the epitome of hegemonic masculinity *per se*. This clash between history and the present can also be illustrated by the release of the big budget film *The Skirmish at Bender* (1983).[43] *The Skirmish at Bender* was a historical comedy in which Gösta Ekman's grandson and namesake, Gösta Ekman, played Charles XII with a mask and in a manner that in fact resembled his grandfather's serious interpretation. But after 60 years, this exaggerated acting style had transformed into, and was now understood as, physical slapstick comedy.

The Skirmish at Bender was also a catastrophic failure at the Swedish box office, while the original *Karl XII* was a blockbuster. There can be no doubt that *Karl XII* tapped into the Swedish historical consciousness of the 1920s in a way that *The Skirmish at Bender* was not able to do. This difference has, consequently, been interpreted in terms of changes in the historical consciousness in Sweden during this 60-year period. The image of Charles XII no longer had the ability to evoke a sense of national honour.[44] But the fact is that *The Skirmish at Bender* was a comedy without any such intentions. The answer to why this film failed could perhaps be found, at least partially, in the fact that it did not tap into the parallel, more popular historical consciousness. But then again, it is a very bad film.

Notes

1. Sverker Oredsson, *Svensk rädsla: Offentlig fruktan i Sverige under 1900-talets första hälft* (Lund: Nordic Academic Press, 2001), pp. 21-39, 95-114, 128-133.
2. Ibid., pp. 21-39, 79-95, 128-133.
3. Lars Åhlander (ed), *Svensk filmografi*, 2, *1920-1929* (Stockholm: Svenska filminstitutet, 1982), p. 242. To limit any confusion, I use the Swedish name of the film (*Karl XII*) and the English name of the king (Charles XII).
4. Swedish title: *Karolinerna*.
5. Ulf Zander, *Fornstora dagar, moderna tider: Bruket av och debatter om svensk historia från sekelskifte till sekelskifte* (Lund: Nordic Academic Press, 2001), pp. 44-48, 115-119, 130-133, 154. Oredsson, *Svensk rädsla*, pp. 36-39.
6. Zander, *Fornstora dagar*, pp. 90-94, 127, 137, 153.
7. The two parts of *Karl XII* premiered on 2 February and 16 November 1925, respectively. Both films are preserved at the Swedish Film Institute.
8. Leif Furhammar, *Filmen i Sverige: En historia i tio kapitel och en fortsättning* (1991; Stockholm: Dialogos/Svenska Filminstitutet, 2003), pp. 114-117; Per Olov Qvist, *Folkhemmets bilder: Modernisering, motstånd och mentalitet i den svenska 30-talsfilmen* (Lund: Arkiv förlag, 1995), pp. 89-96.
9. Åhlander (ed), pp. 242-244.
10. Signature Damsel [Siri Thorngren-Olin], "Karl XII – vår svenska naionalfilm – fullbordad", *Stockholms-Tidningen* 17 November 1925.
11. Signature Hake [Harald Hansen], "En triumf för svensk film", *Svenska Dagbladet* 17 November 1925.
12. Signature Bes [Bernhard Bengtsson], "Filmvärlden", *Folkets Dagblad Politiken* 3 February 1925.
13. Ibid.
14. Tommy Gustafsson, *En fiende till civilisationen: Manlighet, genusrelationer, sexualitet och rasstereotyper i svensk filmkultur under 1920-talet* (Lund: Sekel bokförlag, 2007), pp. 23-26, 212-217. See also, Bo Florin, *Den nationella stilen: Studier i den svenska filmens guldålder* (Stockholm: Aura förlag, 1997).
15. Signature Robin Hood [Bengt Idestam-Almqvist], "'Carl XII' – ett imponerande filmverk", *Stockholms-Tidningen* 3 February 1925.
16. Signature Damsel.
17. Tallak Moland, "Konstruksjon av mandighet i det nordlige landskapet: Om Fridtjof Nansens polarferder ved århundreskiftet", in Anne Marie Berggren (ed), *Manligt och omanligt i ett historiskt perspektiv* (Stockholm: Forskningsrådsnämnden, 1999), pp. 213-221.
18. David Tjeder, "Konsten att blifva herre öfver hvarje lidelse: Den ständigt hotade manligheten", in Berggren (ed), pp. 179-183.
19. Sanimir Resic, *American Warriors in Vietnam: Warrior Values and the Myth of the War Experience During the Vietnam War, 1965-1973* (Lund: Lund University, 1999), p. 8.
20. George L. Mosse, *Fallen Soldiers: Reshaping the Memory of the World Wars* (New York: Oxford University Press, 1990), pp. 80-88, 126-156.
21. Oswald Kuylenstierna, "Karl XII:s-filmen – ett statligt fosterländskt verk", *Aftonbladet* 3 February 1925; signature Robin Hood.
22. R.W. Connell, *Masculinities* (Cambridge: Polity Press, 1995), pp. 76-77.
23. Gustafsson, pp. 172-197. The film's Swedish title is *Carl XII's kurir*.
24. Connell, pp. 78-79.

25. Signature Bes.
26. Tjeder, pp. 183-188.
27. Kuylenstierna.
28. Signature Ax [Axel Andersson], "Filmvärlden", *Folkets Dagblad Politiken* 17 November 1925.
29. Mosse, p. 167.
30. Thomas Sörensen, *Det blänkande eländet: En bok om kronprinsens husarer i sekelskiftets Malmö* (Lund: Lund University, 1997), pp. 65-78.
31. See for example: Biopatrullen, *Arbetet* 3 February 1925; signature Bes; signature Nixon & Partners [Nils Horney and associates], "Karl XII och Kalle Utter i filmupplagor", *Social-Demokraten* 3 February 1925.
32. See for example, Gustaf Cederström, "Karl XII:s-filmen", *Nya Dagligt Allehanda* 17 November 1925; signature Damsel.
33. Mosse, p. 150.
34. For an exception, see for example Cederström.
35. Vladimir Semitjoff, "Två hjältar: Filmens kung Karl och tsar Peter genom ryska ögon", *Film-journalen* 1925 (11).
36. *Arbetet* 24 November 1925.
37. Åhlander (ed), pp. 239, 243-244, 267.
38. Robert Brent Toplin, *Reel History: In Defense of Hollywood* (Lawrence: University Press of Kansas, 2002), p. 42.
39. Mats Jönsson, *Film och historia: Historisk hollywoodfilm 1960-2000* (Lund: KFS, 2004), passim.
40. Tommy Gustafsson, "Filmen som historisk källa: Historiografi, pluralism och representativitet", *Historisk tidskrift* 2006 (3), pp. 482-486.
41. See for example, George G. Iggers, *Historiography in the Twentieth Century: From Scientific Objectivity to the Postmodern Challenge* (Hanover: Wesleyan University Press, 1997).
42. Zander, passim.
43. Swedish title: *Kalabaliken i Bender*, directed by Mats Aréhn.
44. Ibid., p. 342.

Family Matters

The Bernadottes and the 1940 Defence Loan

Mats Jönsson

The founding of the National Board of Information constitutes one of the most important media decisions of the Swedish coalition government during the Second World War. From 26 January 1940 up until the end of the war, this omnipotent institution with close ties to the Foreign Ministry was responsible for all information in and out of the country. Naturally, images passing its massive censorship apparatus became hard currency in the ongoing propaganda activities. The Swedish royal family Bernadotte not only offered an abundance of such sought-after imagery, but also included several members with professional experiences of modern mass media.

It was in 1814 that a French officer in Napoleon's army, Jean Baptiste Bernadotte, became king of Sweden under the name Charles XIV John. Naturally, this appointment meant that the Bernadotte family quickly needed to invent a number of traditions suitable for and expected of a royal family.[1] This predicament might even explain the willingness to interact with the media displayed by future generations of Bernadottes. King Oscar II was, for instance, one of the first persons to ever be filmed in Sweden. The event took place in 1897 when the king arrived at the Art and Industry Exhibition in Stockholm, and these moving regal images turned into one of the most popular media attractions of the entire fair.[2] Oscar's son, King Gustavus V, was also a keen user of and actor in modern mass media, but his children and grandchildren revealed an even more profound and consistent media literacy.

For instance, Prince Wilhelm Bernadotte participated within the media sphere from the 1920s to the 1950s in at least two ways, both as a producer of conservative and nationalistic films, articles and radio programmes and as a sought after royal media celebrity. The latter fact was even commented upon by a film periodical as early as 1927: "Prince Wilhelm has stood in front of more film cameras than most mortals – the Prince of Wales being the exception".[3] Thus, Prince Wilhelm is something of a media paradox in the twentieth century: a reactionary when it came to content, but at the same time fully realizing the value of being absolutely modern in form.[4] Arguably, his initially quite naïve fascination for the film medium therefore constitutes an early insight into the ways in which the power of media was conceived of. Hence, members of the Swedish royal court, such as Prince Wilhelm, clearly understood the significance and attraction of offering themselves as mediated images. And naturally, they predominantly did so in order to ensure continued popularity and position within the public sphere.

Prince Wilhelm's son, Count Lennart Bernadotte, was another medially active Swedish nobility, directing many short films as well as heading a number of public events and activities. Among other things, he was founding editor of the photographic periodical *FOTO* from 1940 onwards, the first president for the National Organization of Film Amateurs in Sweden and sometimes even volunteered as an actor in fiction films. In 1944, Count Lennart even portrayed one of his ancestors in the fiction film *Prince Gustaf*, where he played the part of Crown Prince Carl who in 1859 became King Charles XV. Count Folke Bernadotte is yet another media active member of the Swedish royal family. Among other things, he functioned as head curator and chief-director during one of the largest exhibitions in Stockholm during the Second World War, People and Defence in 1940. King Gustavus V's opening of this exhibition during an official ceremony was actually filmed by Count Lennart and later included as a segment in the short documentary *A Day with the King*, which premiered in the cinemas shortly afterwards. Subsequently, the Bernadottes have often been far more attuned and attentive to media changes and techniques than many other official institutions in Sweden.

In the following, some of these royal images and individuals are under scrutiny, with an emphasis on the staging and depiction of them during the first of the three so-called defence loans (undertaken in 1940, 1941, and 1942, respectively). The concept of "family" is at the centre of the investigation, and the aim is to analyse how ideas, ideals, and images of "family" were implemented in the royal mediation surrounding the first of these three loans.

Loan and Crown

On 25 April 1940, Swedish press and radio announced that a national defence loan was to be launched the following Monday under the supervision of the National Debt Office. The two main incentives to voluntarily loan money to the state by signing war bonds were a four per cent interest rate paid out each year and a full payback on 1 November 1945. As expected, there was no upper limit for how much one individual or institution could lend, but the smallest amount for a single bond was set to 50 Swedish kronor, so that even the financially weakest citizens would be able to participate.

In order to facilitate subscriptions to the loan, bonds were immediately distributed to banks and post offices around the country. Among the organizations legitimizing the launch were labour unions, employers' institutions, national associations, voluntary societies, as well as cooperative groups and committees. Almost immediately, "loan clubs" were spontaneously formed at factories, institutions, and schools, while so-called loan parties surfaced as popular propaganda platforms in most municipalities. In an interview made one week into the campaign, the head of the National Debt Office, Karl Hildebrand, concluded that the organizational work of the defence loan already involved between one and two million citizens (out of a total population of a little under six and a half million).[5] The following year, an official report estimated that the defence loan campaign thus far had resulted in no less than 2,000 meetings around the country, normally with several thousand participants on each separate occasion.[6]

Because of the extensiveness and importance of the defence loan project, a separate propaganda council was established early on. Among others, it included the managing director of Sweden's largest film company Swedish Film Industry (SF), Olof Andersson, the head of Swedish Radio, Carl Anders Dymling, as well as representatives of other commercial, political, journalistic, and social interests.[7] One of the first results of the council was the short compilation film *For Land and Freedom* (1940). Commissioned from Andersson's film company, it can be described as a long commercial for the loan.[8] The Swedish Board of Film Censors – supervised by the National Board of Information – cleared this film for public screening on the very day the first defence loan was launched, 29 April, and thereafter a large number of copies were distributed to local and regional organizations around the country.[9] But the defence loan topic also appeared in the political debate. During the national parliamentary election in September 1940, for instance, the loan was highlighted as an important issue included in the Social Democratic Party's election film *Defence and Welfare of the People*.[10]

My starting point in the present text is that the Swedish defence loan constitutes one of the most thorough, methodical and complex propaganda campaigns ever undertaken in Sweden. Because its main task was to carry the "right" messages across to the citizens, the potential financiers of the loan, the

Frame from the Social Democratic election film, *Defence and Welfare of the People*, 1940.

85

carefully controlled content had an almost exclusively domestic focus – directed inwards towards the actual as well as conceptual centre of the nation. This was largely done in the hope of mobilizing a stronger will to defend two of the most important concepts in Sweden during the war: *freedom* and *independence*. These two symbolically charged words also permeated the defence loan rhetoric, and more often than not they were accompanied by images of the royal family and insignia.[11] In the media, the Bernadottes subsequently came to function as some sort of visual warrants for the continuation, preservation and protection of Sweden's freedom and independence. Just consider the poster closest to the camera in the image above from *Defence and Welfare of the People*. Here, the most well-known symbol of the Swedish monarchy – the three Crowns with more than 600 years of iconic history behind it – guards the nation's freedom and independence in the form of a protective shield of royal heritage.[12]

However, in this context, it needs to be made clear that the Swedish monarchy was neither politically nor medially passive during the war, only acting when and as commanded.[13] On the contrary, and as mentioned in the introduction to this book, the Bernadottes have been far more acceptant of the uses of and presence in the mass media than have most leading Swedish politicians. Moreover, in wartime Sweden, the polysemic nature of the royal imagery quickly became apparent to the political elite. Among the citizenry, the mass-mediated monarchy not only triggered profound memories of heroic royal times of international political power during legendary wars, it also connoted a great national heritage with close links to centuries of peace under the reign of the Bernadottes. The Swedish royal family thus came to function as a kind of ritualistic constant in a time of severe turbulence. And as has been convincingly proven with regard to a fundamentally different royal milieu and period, most rituals are "deliberately unaltered so as to give an impression of continuity, community and comfort, despite overwhelming contextual evidence to the contrary."[14]

King Gustavus V was the most frequently employed ritualistic symbol of the Swedish Crown during World War Two, and consequently he was the first Swede to sign on for the defence loan in 1940. The event made all the major newspapers, which reported that the king had signed on for the impressive sum of 250,000 Swedish kronor.[15] But the rest of the royal family had also contributed and among those mentioned were the Crown Prince, the Heir Presumptive, Prince Charles as well as royal funds such as the Jubilee Funds for Oscar II and Gustavus V, and the Eighty Years Fund for Gustavus V. A week later, readers also learnt that the Memorial Fund for the Crown Princess had contributed an additional 50,000 kronor, while Prince Wilhelm had signed on for half of that sum.[16] Many newspapers underlined that the Bernadottes together had lent more than half a million kronor during the first few weeks of the campaign. In other words, this time the royal family not only sanctioned the defence loan figuratively in the form of symbols and signs, but also supported it in real financial figures. This, in turn, indicates that the monarchy was well aware that their normal ritualistic appearances now needed to be combined with more active participation than usual. The official royal manoeuvres were thus not just self-conscious, but in many ways also self-initiated and self-staged, launching the Bernadottes as patriotic figure heads of the family of Sweden.[17]

Naturally, such a big national family needed something large and great to gather around, which might explain why the defence loan was immediately hailed in the press as the largest loan ever undertaken in Sweden.[18] The paradoxical aspect of celebrating that the state needed large sums of money from its citizens in order to defend itself also became apparent a month later, when one of the most high-profiled performances for the first defence loan was staged at the open-air museum Skansen on Royal Djurgården in Stockholm.[19] A number of senior members of the royal family attended this prestigious occasion, hereby giving both themselves and the event credence and legitimacy. Additionally, the presence of prominent politicians, militaries, and media further underlined the crucial nature of the occasion. Thus, not only was it imperative to give the general public the impression that almost all leading members of the national family had gathered here. It was of equal importance that the sinister issue at hand be presented as something positive to celebrate. One article skilfully combined these two emotional polarities by including photographs of the crown prince, the minister of defence as well as the famous tenor Jussi Björling and the celebrated actor Anders de Wahl. In some ways, this ad could be seen as an early example of what later came to be known as *politainment*.[20]

Article about the so-called Defence Party at Skansen, with photos of royalty, politics and culture. *Svenska Dagbladet* 17 May 1940.

A commentator in one of the domestic newsreels of the time adopted a similar kind of rhetoric, highlighting the celebratory nature of the Skansen event by calling it "The Big Propaganda and Citizen Party for the Defence Loan", at the same time as the royal presence also was emphasized: "60,000 citizens lead by the crown prince had gathered here".[21] But the crown prince did not just lead his fellow members of the national family to this party ritual; he also held a speech that was broadcast on national radio between 9.40 and 10.00 pm.[22] His royal message was fully in line with the standard defence-loan rhetoric, emphasizing the need for quick financial help and concluding that by helping the state "we help ourselves, our homes, *our freedom and independence*, and all that we hold dear in this world."[23] No doubt, this speech strengthened the heritage aura of the ongoing campaign via its verbal content and the ways in which it was communicated. That is, from a royal mouth, on a public platform, at a classic site, according to a well-known ritual, within a festive framework, and with a majority of the country's elite and mass media present.

In this context, it needs to be mentioned that the festive framework normally surrounding the defence loan was sometimes met by quite harsh criticism in the media. Shortly before the event at Skansen, for instance, one reviewer attacked a radio programme about the defence loan because it "pushed the real images into a theatrical arrangement with recitation, music and chronicle reading [...] in the hope of hereby influencing sentimental souls".[24] This quote is of importance for a number of reasons. One has to do with the fact that it is a radio transmission that is criticized here. For no matter how important live events such as the one at Skansen actually were, most messages about saving money to defend the Swedish realm were spread with the help of modern mass media. Thus, the prime targets of the loan propaganda were not citizens present in person at each specific occasion, but everyone listening to the radio, reading the newspapers and watching the films.[25] Accordingly, alterations in uses and techniques of modern means of communication played a crucial part when traditional words and images addressed contemporary issues. Or, as John B. Thompson has described it:

> the decline of traditional authority and the traditional grounding of action does not spell the demise of tradition but rather signals a shift in its nature and role, as individuals come to rely more and more on mediated and delocalized traditions as a means of making sense of the world and of creating a sense of belonging.[26]

Ad and Heritage

Based on the above, it is not surprising that the Bernadottes' media skill surfaced as a crucial factor in propaganda aimed at creating a sense of belonging in Sweden. Their media competence became particularly evident in the ways in which they related to and skilfully reused the dominant discourses of the time. The crown prince's speech at Skansen was, for instance, both inspired by and quoted from the initial, and most famous, advertisement for the Swedish defence loan. This advertisment was published in all major newspapers on the first day of the loan, 29 April 1940, and also occurred later in other versions as well as in the form of posters and leaflets. Part of its original message reads as follows:

> Swedish Men and Women! Our defence needs your financial contribution. Sweden does not threaten anyone. But we want to guard that which we hold most precious: our native country, our paternally inherited freedom, our right to independence, our culture – the fruit of millenniums of cultivation – our language, our homes, our children, and our future. Everyone ought to feel it as his or her bidding duty to, each according to ability, participate in the defence loan that hereby is offered. This plea is now spreading all across the country. Let us hope that it will work as a wake-up call and an incentive to mutual action.[27]

In wartime Sweden, it must have been almost impossible not to consider oneself as a receiver of this message, that is, as belonging to the national family addressed here. But although this is an inclusive – and originally perhaps even an intentionally all-inclusive message – there is undoubtedly an implicit threat underlying the splendid varnish of carefully polished patriotism.[28] To some extent, the narrative strategy at work here can be summarized using the "carrot and stick" idiom. On the one hand, we have the overall idea of a greater good, the carrot, emphasizing that every small sacrifice is as important as all the larger loans – present pains will result in future gains.[29] These emotionally charged references are not least obvious in connection with "that which we hold most precious" (country, *freedom*, *independence*, home, culture). On the other hand, we have the proverbial stick, authoritatively making it clear that those who did not contribute would find themselves outside that which the majority of their peers and leaders were struggling so hard to defend – namely freedom and independence.[30] These betrayers would of course still be physically included within the country's borders, but

Advertisement for the Defence Loan published in all major Swedish newspapers in 1940.

psychologically they were facing an exclusion from the national family unit of severe and profound proportions.

The design of the ad visually strengthened these allusions to an enhanced nationalism with the help of the royal insignia and signs. For instance, the framing banner consists of the classic three-crown symbol. Together with a similar but large one in the middle of the picture, it is, however, the sword held by two hands that attracts most of our attention. Three days before the ad was published, newspapers revealed that this image was inspired by a famous sculpture by the renowned Swedish artist Carl Eldh.[31] The motif was none other than the legendary Engelbrekt Engelbrektsson, who not only headed a peasant rebellion against the Scandinavian King Eric of Pomerania in 1434, but who also, the following year at what by many is regarded as the first Swedish parliament, was elected Captain of the Swedish Realm.[32]

In some respects, this title gave Engelbrekt more power than the foreign king, which over the centuries has turned him into the prime Swedish symbol for a democratically elected head of state. For instance, the 500 anniversary of his legendary election was celebrated in 1935, when King Gustavus V unveiled Eldh's sculpture at an official ceremony. Images from this iconic public ritual repeatedly resurfaced in the media, and just as with the monarchy, different parties on the political scale saw the potential of this polysemic output. Not only do we find images form this ceremony in an election film for the Conservative Party in 1938, *The Country You Must Protect*, they are also included in the formerly mentioned propaganda film for the 1940 defence loan, *For Land and Freedom*, which, indirectly via the National Board of Information, was commissioned by the coalition government lead by the Social Democrats.[33]

But the Engelbrekt saga also reached the general public in other ways. In September 1940, for instance, the play "The Man of Freedom" premiered at yet another festivity for the defence loan at Skansen. According to one of the producers, this play was staged in the era of Engelbrekt because "the aim of the performance is to remind contemporary Swedes of the great heritage of freedom we now have to administrate."[34] In the last of the three defence loan campaigns, the Labour Movement's own film company Filmo produced a short film, *We are Thousands* (1942), which depicts the youth organization of the Social Democratic Party.[35] In one section, we see how young party members perform an historical play at an outdoor camp that partly deals with the Engelbrekt rebellion of 1434. Famous words from the oath he swore are even quoted by the film's voice-over.[36]

Within powerful sections of Swedish politics, and most specifically among leading Social Democrats such as Prime Minister Per Albin Hansson, Engelbrekt thus came to symbolize the origin of democratic freedom and parliamentarianism. In fact, already in the mid-1930s, Hansson had hailed him as "the creator of a national conscience and the father of the people's community".[37] In some respects, this quote indicates that the Social Democrats saw Engelbrekt as a forerunner to and honorary member of the People's Home – the dominant national metaphor for the Swedish welfare state ever since it had been re-launched by Hansson in

1928.[38] As a national symbol for a "royal democracy" of sorts, Engelbrekt thus can be said to have effectively sanctioned the ongoing union between the Social Democratic Party and the monarchy that was taking place during the war.[39] For by mixing legendary figures of monarchic dimensions such as Engelbrekt with living royalties such as the Bernadottes, the political elite strengthened the probability of an all-inclusive national family with the Crown in the centre.

The ideologically initiated strategy of using the ancient Engelbrekt for contemporary propaganda purposes by no means constituted an exception. On the contrary, the official rhetoric of modernizing Sweden's armed forces repeatedly employed images of old to get messages of novelty across to the masses.[40] And at a time when the fate of the country was uncertain after recent invasions of the rest of the Nordic countries, it seems only logical that symbols of a well-known and legendary past surfaced as helpful sources of comfort. In other words, the audiovisual output in wartime Sweden did not follow the standard procedures of social representation, where new or unintelligible information is normally first anchored in prevailing systems of knowledge and meaning, whereafter it is objectified in various intelligible ways.[41]

Instead, one could argue that the people in charge of the Swedish defence loan campaigns consciously chose to primarily anchor already well-known images of a royal past even deeper within the collective memory of the nation. And although the belief in a continued "neutral royal democracy of Sweden" was mainly a utopian self-conception, it nevertheless turned into a constitutional mantra and a symbolic locus within which many citizens felt secure and at home. And here, mediated references to patriotic rebels in medieval times like Engelbrekt and to the long peaceful reign under the Bernadottes surely helped to reinforce this belief. The well-anchored and well-known iconography of the Crown became something to cling to when everything else around seemed to be on the verge of collapsing. However, this meant that it became increasingly important for leading politicians to include the royal family within the frames of the ever-expanding People's Home.

Home and Gender

Many were the paths towards such inclusions. An already established path was to reinforce citizens' seemingly personal ties to the royals by displaying the private quarters of the Crown in the media. Throughout the twentieth century, this kind of royal performance has been depicted, and during World War Two, the Swedish royal family was already well accustomed to such coverage. An example of this was published in the daily newspaper *Svenska Dagbladet* in October 1940, and it dealt with one of the homes of the crown prince and crown princess, Ulriksdal's Castle. The rhetorical significances of the home metaphor, of mixing the past with the future, and of a strong need for family unity in wartime Sweden are all apparent in this article. Not least when it is concluded that the photographs from the castle "give a glimpse of the dear, royal

- en hela folkets bilderbok

VÅR KUNGAFAMILJ

Detta ståtliga praktalbum

som i 160 bilder med utförlig text skildrar vår kunga-
familjs liv i vardag och helg år årets utan jämförelse yp-
persta och intressantaste bilderbok. Vi få följa vår kunga-
familjs öden från kung Gustafs födelse år 1858 fram till
och med 1940 och se glimtar ur samtliga Bernadotters liv
under denna långa tid. Speglad i deras öden under mer
än åtta decennier få vi också möta svensk historia under
denna tidrymd som mer än kanske någon betyder en om-
vandling av det svenska samhället. De texter som beled-
saga det rika, omväxlande bildmaterialet ha särskilt ta-
git sikte på dessa omständigheter, och bidraga i hög
grad att stärka vår tillit och förtröstan i den prövande tid
vi alla genomleva.

Denna bilderbok är en beredskapsbok.

Varje svensk för vilken fosterlandets
frihet och oberoende under vårt eget
fritt valda styrelsesätt alltjämt är en
hjärtesak, kan hämta glädje och upp-
muntran ur detta verk

— **bör**   I alla bok- och tidningsaffärer.
                                    Pris Kronor 2: 50.

och får ej
saknas i
något svenskt
hem!

Advertisement for a royal photo-album, published in *Svenska Dagbladet* 8 November 1940.

home, where tradition and modernity are united in an unusually harmonious way."[42] Another representative illustration of mediated intimacy with the Swedish Crown occurred around the same time, but now in the form of ads for a new photo album of the Bernadotte family. Here, the political ambition of including everyone under the roof of the People's Home was expressed as follows: "All class boundaries are erased when it comes to the interest in our revered royal family, and the album with the royals thus becomes a picture book for the entire population."[43]

In this context, it is obvious that one cannot – and should not – oversee gender issues when examining the media's efforts to make Swedish royals appear more personal and private in the public sphere. Ever since the late seventeenth century, Sweden has been incarnated by a woman, Mother Svea, who is normally portrayed with a crown on her head.[44] An example of her continued validity during World War Two was published the day before the launch of the first defence loan. Under a drawing of Mother Svea collecting money from Swedish citizens, in what usually is seen as her horn of plenty, it was explicitly underlined that the comforting mother of the nation was this time actually in desperate need of funding from her "sons" in order to make "our home" a better place.[45]

Naturally, the day-to-day life of Mother Svea's "daughters" was also displayed and discussed in the media during the war. Seen as one homogenous group, these women became known as "the spiritual home guard" of the country, and their efforts in their private households were frequently compared to activities in the overall household of the nation. Throughout the war, the voluntary and charity work of "the spiritual home guard" therefore surfaced as important nodes of patriotism on the domestic arena. One of the most central organizations was "Active Housekeeping", a governmental initiative launched by the above-mentioned National Board of Information in June 1940. Its main objective was to rationalize domestic issues and make them more effective and – perhaps even more importantly – more publicly know.[46] On many occasions, the media explicitly singled out female nobilities within the royal family as active or even founding members of these organizations.[47] For instance, Crown Princess Margareta's Female Home Guard Fund, which had not been in use since World War One, once again came into force in 1940.[48] While Princess Sibylla, owing to her well-known interest in driving, was elected honorary chairman for Stockholm's Car Association for Women.[49]

Another example of how royal gender played a significant role in strengthening the Swedish belief in home and family was published on 12 May 1940, that is, only two weeks into the first defence loan campaign. The article, "Royal Mothers in the War Zone", concluded that the most important thing for a royal lady in Europe at this point in time was "the duty to, together with the population of the country, share the dangers of war, and with a calm and balanced posture, to carry the heavy burden of being an example."[50] In other words, the need for compulsory sacrifices by everyone, including royals, was presented with the help of emotionally charged stories about these female celebrities. Indeed, the article was even accompanied by a photo gallery in the hope of enhancing the identification with six of these royal mothers: Queen Wilhelmina of Holland, Queen Dowager Mary of England, Arch-Duchess Charlotte of Luxemburg, the Crown Princess Juliana of Holland, Queen Dowager Elsabet of Belgium, and Ex-Empress Hermine of Prussia.

Article about "Royal Mothers in the War Zone". *Dagens Nyheter* 12 May 1940.

But the Swedish readers were also brought closer to home in this article, learning about the hardships that Crown Princess Ingrid of Denmark (originally daughter of the crown prince of Sweden) had faced with regard to her newborn daughter, and about how Crown Princess Märtha of Norway had been forced to flee the Norwegian capital to find a safe haven for her young ones.

Subsequently, royal personas from other countries were also used in the ongoing domestication of Sweden and its citizens. And sometimes the efforts of trying to make Swedish readers more familiar with foreign royals took even more sensational turns. One such example was published around the same time, that is, in mid-May 1940. It was entitled "Court Gossip about the Entire Family from Victoria to George VI" and consisted of a review of a book about the British court that recently had been translated into Swedish.[51] The best parts of the book were said to be those dealing with gossip about foreign courts, because in these sections "plebeians outside are actually allowed to attend even when the 'most daring' secrets are revealed".[52] Given their central symbolic function during the war, articles, radio programmes, and films containing similar intimate gossip about the Bernadottes never occurred in the public sphere. The Swedish royal family had another and substantially different role to play – and that was as iconic example of patriotism in the *intra*national media rhetoric.

End Perspectives

In many ways, the Swedish defence loan campaign of 1940 seems to be indicative of a larger wartime propaganda apparatus saturating every level of society. Indeed, I would even go so far as to suggest that the symbolic and literal efforts of holding the neutral realm of Sweden together have rarely been so openly displayed and hailed in the media as during World War Two. For instance, the recurring emphasis in the media on "family" and "home" made it almost impossible for Swedish citizens to exclude themselves from the People's Home that was still under construction. And because the media output about this all-encompassing home predominantly pointed inwards towards the centre of this imagined community, the idea of a national family harbouring everyone surfaced as a particularly useful metaphor in wartime Sweden.[53]

A significant reason for its success was the unique collaboration between a coalition government led by the Social Democrats, on the one hand, and a medially trained royal family, on the other. Together, these two powerful institutions moulded the Swedish nation into one big family with the help of images, words, and performances that were launched almost everywhere and on a daily basis. Whether or not this media bombardment meant continued freedom and independence for the country is difficult to establish from a brief study such as this. But it surely contributed to Sweden staying out of the war, which, albeit ethically dubious, was the whole purpose of the loan in the first place.

That the royal *family* was in the centre of this propaganda is therefore of the utmost importance. Especially because the family concept effectively boiled down Swedish society into one patriotic formula that was easily understood by everyone and easy to use by most political parties. On a collective level, "the family" constituted a well-known metaphor thanks to the success of the People's Home and decades of Bernadotte imagery. On an individual level, however, "the family" turned out to be an equally convenient trope, partly detectable in the extent to which the royal family's members appeared in the public sphere, but also evident in the ways in which Swedish citizens saw the intimate tales about the monarchy as mediated invitations into the private lives of the Crown. Together with royal radio speeches heard in most Swedish homes and the royal film images screened in the local cinemas, recurring visits to the homes and photo albums of the Bernadottes thus helped to firmly position the monarchy in the middle of the national home. This, in turn, indicates that the Swedish royal family in many ways can be conceived of as "both queen and prisoner" during the Second World War, not just entrapped within the official idea of an expanding People's Home, but also caught in the media coverage of their own private domains.[54]

The claim that "to be a symbol, and an effective symbol, you must be vividly and often seen" consequently seems to have been just as relevant for the Swedish monarchy during World War Two as it was for Queen Victoria of England in the late nineteenth century and still is for royals today.[55] Therefore, when a recent study concludes that the Swedish monarchy is "a royal house of adaptability", this actually is an accurate and, with regard to their relations to the media, mainly positive description of the Bernadottes and their actions during the launch of the first Swedish defence loan in 1940.[56]

Notes

1. Indeed, the strategies behind and results of the launching of the Bernadottes in Sweden have been analysed in an extensive research project. See, for instance, Mikael Alm & Britt-Inger Johansson (eds), *Scripts of Kingship: Essays on Bernadotte and Dynastic Formation in an Age of Revolution* (Uppsala: Department of History, 2008).

2. About this fair and the entire Stockholm exhibition of 1897, see Anders Ekström, Solveig Jülich & Pelle Snickars (eds), *1897: Mediehistorier kring Stockholmsutställningen* (Stockholm: SLBA, 2006).

3. Unsigned, "De kungliga och filmen", *Svensk skolfilm och bildningsfilm* 1927 (31).

4. For a discussion on Prince Wilhelm see, Pelle Snickars, "Bildrutor i minnets film: Om medieprins Wilhelm och film som käll- och åskådningsmaterial", in Pelle Snickars & Cecilia Trenter (eds), *Det förflutna som film och vice versa: Om medierade historiebruk* (Lund: Studentlitteratur, 2004), as well as, Pelle Snickars, "Prins Wilhelm och politikens medialisering" *Ord & bild* 2006 (1). The issue of *Ord & bild* had Prince Wilhelm as a theme, thus, other articles are about him as well.

5. "Försvarslånet organiseras nu", *Dagens Nyheter* 3 May 1940.

6. *Frihet och försvar: Boken om vår beredskap*, (Stockholm: Esselte, 1941), p. 453.

7. "Historiskt svärd", *Dagens Nyheter* 26 April 1940.

8. Swedish title, *För land och frihet*. This film was based on an election film, *The Land You Must Protect* (*Landet du ska värna*, 1938), which was produced for the Conservative Party during the election campaign in 1938. See, Bengt Bengtsson, "Regionfilmen och konstruktionen av folkhemmet", in Mats Jönsson & Pelle Snickars (eds), *Medier och politik: Om arbetarrörelsens mediestrategier under 1900-talet* (Stockholm: SLBA, 2007), pp.148–152. When launching the second defence loan in 1941, the council commissioned a new film from SF, *The Warg Family* (*Familjen Warg*).

9. This distribution was, at least, undertaken until March 1941. See censor card no. 61452, 29 April 1940, at the Swedish Board of Film Censors (Statens biografbyrå), which was also under the supervision of the National Board of Information during the war.

10. Swedish title, *Folkets värn och välfärd*.

11. That these two words dominated the overall political agenda became evident in connection witrh the May Day Parade in 1940, which was substituted with "The Citizen Parade for Freedom and Independence".

12. About the real impact and symbolic importance of the royal shield during World War Two, see Mats Jönsson, "'Den kungliga skölden': Per Albin Hansson, Gustaf V och medierna", in Jönsson & Snickars (eds), 2007, pp. 159-206.

13. For instance, just around the period of the launch of the defence loan, King Gustavus V undertook a private and highly controversial correspondence with the German chancellor Adolf Hitler concerning the continued neutrality of Sweden. See, for instance, *Göteborgs Handels- och Sjöfarts-Tidning* 7 May 1940 and *Sydsvenska Dagbladet* 7 May 1940.

14. David Cannadine, "The Context, Performance and Meaning of Ritual: The British Monarchy and 'The Invention of Tradition', c. 1820-1977", in Eric Hobsbawm & Terence Ranger (eds), *The Invention of Tradition* (Cambridge: Cambridge University Press, 1983), p. 105.

15. See, for instance, "Kungen var den förste som tecknade andel: Över en halv million från det kungliga huset", *Svenska Dagbladet* 30 April 1940; "Försvarslånet får god start, kungliga huset har köpt obligationer för en halv miljon", *Göteborgs Handels- och Sjöfarts-Tidning* 29 April 1940; "Kungen först på försvarslånet", *Aftonbladet* 29 April 1940; and "Försvarslånet hade en lyckad premiär, Konungen tecknade för 250.000 kr.", *Sydsvenska Dagladet* 30 April 1940. Later on, at the end of the first defence loan, the press announced that the king had made an additional contribution of 150,000 Swedish kronor. "Även konungen deltar i försvarslånets spurt", *Dagens Nyheter* 26 October 1940. The largest contribution during the first defence loan was made by the Scandinavian Bank, which signed on for 25 million kronor on 28 September 1940.

16. "En jämn ström av köpare gick hela dagen till riksgäldskontoret", *Dagens Nyheter* 30 April 1940.

17. The press also underlined the idea of equality behind this national action and hailed the first defence loan as a "patriotic loan" and a "real people's loan". "Staten lånar ½ milliard för försvaret: Patriotiskt 4% lån framlägges inom kort: Förmedlas av 31 organisationer", *Svenska Dagbladet* 25 April 1940.

18. Ibid.

19. Ever since it was established in 1891, Skansen has been the most frequently used arena by the Bernadottes and during the war it was a recurrent platform for various defence matters.

20. Andreas Dörner, *Politainment: Politik in der medialen Erlebnisgesellschaft* (Frankfurt am Main: Suhrkamp, 2001).

21. "Svensk Filmindustris Revy", newsreel no 35, May 1940. Even the sinister Swedish Board of Film Censors described this event in optimistic terms, calling it "the defence party at Skansen" on the back of one of its censor cards. See censor card no. 61513, 27 May 1940.

22. "Radioprogrammet", *Folkets Dagblad* 25 April 1940.

23. "Kronprins Gustaf Adolf vädjar till svenska folket", *Minnesboxen 1940: Musiken, händelserna, företeelserna, stämningen…* (Stockholm: Sveriges Radio/Screen Air Television AB, 1999). (My italics.)

24. Signature Fale Bure, "Radio-rapsodi", *Göteborgs Handels- och Sjöfarts-Tidning* 21 May, 1940.

25. This, in turn, explains the power of institutions such as the National Board of Information and the propaganda committee for the defence loan.

26. John B. Thompson, *The Media and Modernity: A Social Theory of the Media* (Cambridge: Polity Press, 1999) p. 187.

27. See, for instance, *Dagens Nyheter* and *Svenska Dagbladet* 29 April 1940.

28. This is one of many wartime versions of the "you are either with us or against us" ultimatum, albeit subtly disguised as the more benevolent "together we stand, divided we fall" parole.

29. Or, as it was formulated in an article published on the very day the first defence loan was made public: "Save for yourself – and you are a patriot!" "Teckna försvarslån lika lätt som att utkvittera ett Rek.", *Svenska Dagbladet* 26 April 1940.

30. This kind of sinister rhetoric predominantly appeared when Swedish politicians addressed the public. One such example occurred when the Minister of Finance, Ernst Wigforss, made a speech on national radio on the evening of the launch of the first loan. The speech, "Defence loan and thrift" ("Försvarslån och sparsamhet"), focused on facts, figures and present

political issues, and was later published as a 15-page leaflet, Ernst Wigforss, *Försvarslån och sparsamhet* (Stockholm: Tidens förlag, 1940).

31. See, for instance, "Historiskt svärd", *Dagens Nyheter* 26 April 1940 and *Svenska Dagbladet* 26 April 1940.

32. Åsa Linderborg, *Socialdemokraterna skriver historia: Historieskrivning som ideologisk maktresurs 1892-2000* (Stockholm: Atlas, 2001), pp. 275-285.

33. The Swedish title of the election film for the Conservative Party was *Landet du ska värna*. Shortly before the defence loan was launched, Engelbrekt was even used as a defence symbol when a new law for the National Home Guard in Sweden was discussed. See, for instance, "Man ur huse till försvar som förr under Engelbrekt", *Göteborgs Handels- och Sjöfarts-Tidning* 22 April 1940.

34. "Luftvärn ger fond åt drama", *Dagens Nyheter* 13 September 1940.

35. Swedish title, *Vi äro tusenden*.

36. This camp was not a small and periphery event of the time. For instance, the key speaker was none other than the Social Democratic Prime Minister Per Albin Hansson, who also appears in the film.

37. Linderborg, p. 282.

38. Originally, the People's Home was a conservative idea in Sweden, emphasizing an unaltered nation based on ancient traditions and a preserved class society with the king as continued leader of the nation.

39. About this powerful union, see Jönsson, in Jönsson & Snickars (eds), 2007, pp. 159–206.

40. See, for instance, Yvonne Hirdman, *Att lägga livet tillrätta: Studier i svensk folkhemspolitik* (Stockholm: Carlssons, 1989), pp. 25–30.

41. Serge Miscovici, *Social Representation: Exploration in Social Psychology* (Cambridge: Polity Press, 2000).

42. Unsigned, "Hos kronprinsparet på Ulriksdal", *Svenska Dagbladet* 6 October 1940.

43. Advertisement, "En hela folkets bilderbok", *Svenska Dagbladet* 9 September 1940.

44. See Anu Koivunen, "Moderns kropp, fädrens land: Nationell film som könsteknologi", in Tytti Soila (ed), *Dialoger: Feministisk filmteori i praktik* (Stockholm: Aura, 1997).

45. Signature HIC, "Det stora lånet", *Dagens Nyheter* 28 April 1940.

46. Johanna Overud, *I beredskap med Fru Lojal: Behovet av kvinnlig arbetskraft i Sverige under andra världskriget* (Stockholm: Almqvist & Wiksell, 2005), especially pp. 176–211.

47. One such example is "The Gift Committee of the Crown Princess", with its eleven district committees. See, for instance, "Till stickorna på nytt!", *Svenska Dagbladet* 28 April 1940. The Committee for Enhanced Female Representation was another important institution of the time. It represented more than 40 separate organizations, was imperative in the propaganda for lending money to the state, and its first national meeting was held before the defence loan campaign started. See signature Attis [Astrid Ljungström], "Hur ska vi spara åt landet?", *Svenska Dagbladet* 22 April 1940.

48. Signature B., "Mobiliseringsorder till alla stickkunniga svenska kvinnor", *Svenska Dagbladet* 5 June 1940.

49. "Stort intresse for kvinnliga bilkåren", *Aftonbladet* 25 April 1940.

50. "Kungliga mödrar i krigszonen", *Dagens Nyheter* 12 May 1940.

51. Charles Devienne, "Hovskvaller om tjocka släkten från Victoria till Georg [sic!] VI", *Göteborgs Handels- och Sjöfarts-Tidning* 18 May 1940. The book was also reviewed in other Swedish newspapers, see, for instance, Harald Schiller, "Kungligt familjeliv i gamla dagar", *Sydsvenska Dagbladet* 1 May 1940.

52. Devienne, 1940.

53. Benedict Anderson, *Imagined Communities: Reflections on the Origin and Spread of Nationalism* (London & New York: Verso, 1991).

54. Michael J. Shapiro, "The Politics of the 'Family'", in Judy Dean (ed), *Cultural Studies and Political Theory* (Ithaca & London: Cornell University Press, 2000), p. 276. Here, Shapiro is quoting Jacques Donzelot and his *The Policing of Families*.

55. Cannadine, p. 119.
56. Guido Knopp, *Majestät! Die letzten großen Monarchien* (München: Bertelsmann, 2006), p. 25.

National Pleasure

Gender and Nation in Royal Yearbooks

Cecilia Åse

The motto chosen by King Carl XVI Gustaf as he ascended the throne in September 1973 reads: "For Sweden – with the times".[1] The phrase contains an ambiguity in the sense that while the Swedish monarchy is regularly depicted as one of the world's oldest and most established, it is simultaneously described as genuinely modern. Underlying this assumption of modernity is clearly the constitutional changes of the early 1970s that ripped the king of his formal political powers, as well as the abolishment a decade later of male privilege to the throne. However, understandings of gender-equality and modernity tend to be put forward not only as central features of the Swedish monarchy, but also as determining aspects of Swedish national identity, of what and who "we" are.[2]

Drawing on feminist theory in relation to gender and nation, my focus in the present article is on how representations of gender, sexuality and the female body are intertwined with constructions of national identity in Swedish discourse on monarchy. In defiance of assertions of modernity and gender neutrality, feminist research has highlighted the fact that all nations are gendered and that gender relations often have been the symbolic site of nationalist constructions and struggles.[3] In my view, the king and queen, and constitutional monarchy in itself, are powerful representations of body and nation, as well as of national community and identity. But how does the institution of monarchy connect representations of national identity to gender?

The female body has regularly been used as a symbol of the nation, thereby feminizing and sexualizing the national community.[4] As Joan B. Landes argues, male political comradeship and political equality between men has been construed through a collective male desire for the symbolic female figure that embodies the nation.[5] However, if we consider the king as an embodied symbol of the Swedish nation, then the understanding of national community as feminized, as embodied by a desirable female figure, may have to be modified. What symbolic position is attributed to the female body in Swedish discourse on monarchy? And how is this position negotiated in relation to issues of reproduction and sexuality as well as to issues of nationalism and national consolidation?

Following Michael Billig, my point of departure is that monarchy cannot be divorced from nationalism.[6] Royal families and dynasties have historically been important in creating the "imagined communities" of contemporary Europe.[7] Royalty is commonly associated with tradition, heritage, and national belonging. These are all important facets of the historical processes underlying nation-building and national consolidation. Nowadays, the royal family and the institution of monarchy can rightly be seen as part of contemporary Swedish everyday life. They are (out) there (everywhere), in the tabloids, on the coins and stamps and regularly on television, be it in connection with the Nobel Prize ceremony, the celebration of 6 June, or in the annual Christmas specials. In this sense, monarchy is part of what Billig terms "banal nationalism", the not-thought-of daily reproduction of a naturalized sense of the nation and of national belonging.[8]

With a focus on how representations of body, gender and sexuality are intertwined with representations of nation, national belonging and community, a number of royal yearbooks and anniversary publications published from 1973 to 2000 will be analysed in the following text. These publications are produced in close connection with the court, photographed and written by journalists that regularly follow and report on royal life.[9] Information on state visits and travels abroad as well as various inaugurations and medal presentations is mixed with details of birthday celebrations, dinner parties and pictures of the royal children playing with their pets. The perspective in the yearbooks is retrospective, the year that has passed being in focus, and photographs dominate over text. The actual content can be characterized as banal and emotional, the tone of the texts being familiarizing and almost intimate.

The analysis focuses on constructions of gender and nation that constantly recur and structure representations of royal life in the yearbooks and anniversary publications. The material analysed is characterized by a conventional framing as well as by the fact that feelings of loyalty and community are enacted. Royal life is visualized and displayed, and the public is called upon to join in. However, while the books describe details of what members of the royal family have been up to – the king going elk-hunting, for example, or the queen wearing a spotted outfit – I would argue that it is not the elk or the spots themselves that are actually conveyed. How many elks were actually brought down or what the pattern of the outfit actually was is certainly not important in my analysis. What is crucial is the ways in which information is conveyed, contextualized, visualized, and interpreted in relation to different facets of gender and nation.

Reproduction and Childbirth

The constitutional monarchy, as a form of government, is dependent upon the royal family successfully reproducing itself. As head of state, the king symbolizes the Swedish nation. His position, duties, and symbolical status are inherited by his direct heirs under conditions that are stipulated in the order of succession from 1810.[10] Heredity and bloodlines defining the succession to the throne imply that the survival of constitutional monarchy is dependent on the king successfully engaging in conjugal relations and royal children actually being born. As the parentage of the offspring has to be vouched for, monarchy clearly also builds upon the control of women's sexuality and reproduction.

Given the constitutional fact that royal blood determines the succession to the Swedish throne, it is not surprising that great public interest surrounds questions of royal conception and childbirth. The delivery of royal babies is deeply ritualized: the queen chooses a birth-witness, the newborn is presented to the government, and a salute is given. One jubilee publication describes the birth of an heir to the crown as a significant national event.

> A baby boy was deeply longed for – both at the Haga castle where there were already four girls and throughout the monarchy of Sweden that still had male succession. A line of direct communication was set up between court-marshal baron von Uggla and salute-batteries all over the country. The baron had his hand on the telephone and at 10:21 the canons were fired from Stockholm, Gothenburg and Karlskrona, from Vaxholm and Härnösand and from all the major Swedish naval warships, wherever they were. Everywhere two 42 round salutes were fired. A girl would have given only one round of 42 shots. When the 43rd shot was fired people started to cheer: – Hurrah, it is a boy![11]

Moreover, pregnancies are depicted as matters of national interest, and the national community is ascribed a sense of care and devotion in relation to the pregnant body.[12] When royal children are born, a sense of collective national pride and happiness is enacted: "Not just mummy and daddy, King Carl XVI Gustaf and Queen Silvia, rejoiced on this happy occasion. The whole Swedish people rejoiced with them. At last a real princess was born!"[13] The event is also tied to national pride in relation to other countries. The world is supposed to have been waiting: "the birth of a royal child was announced to the world."[14] Photographs portraying the young family are ascribed international interest and in "one single afternoon" pictures of the "happy family" were spread around the globe, the "happy family" now being a fact that the "whole world" was to learn about.[15]

It is clear that the female body here is a means for the survival of the monarchy as well as a means for the creation of a sense of national identity and belonging, for a sense of a national "we". Royal childbirths tie the royal family closely to the nation: royal reproduction in this sense also entails the reproduction of conceptions of the nation. Women's bodies are clearly a prerequisite of this double reproduction, of the monarchy as well as the nation. However, women's relation to the nation and their status as national reproducers is marked by ambivalence. Women who are married into the royal family and give birth to royal children are incorporated into the nation through a husband. It is by marriage that her body and the children she gives birth to are regarded as issues of national interest.[16] The woman's biological contribution to the child is often played down or made invisible in the discourse on royalty.[17] An often-reproduced official picture of a 1946 royal christening can be seen as a case in point. The picture portrays four generations of royal men. The women, including the mother of the baby boy, are not in the picture at all. The fact that this is a male genealogy being reproduced is evident, and visually it is almost overwhelmingly male.

The royal male geneaology. Reprint from *Femtio år med kungen: Från lillprins till monark* (1996). *Photo:* Jessica Lund/The National Library of Sweden.

This genealogy is also enacted at occasions such as ceremonies surrounding the coming of age of future heads of state: "Your Majesty, dear daddy ... is how the crown princess commenced her first speech in the Hall of State at Stockholm Royal Palace".[18] On these occasions, motherhood is reduced to an intermediary link between different generations of monarchs.

Women's bodies are heavily inscribed into nationalist discourse and the individual woman's body and subjectivity are immersed into the collective national body. While women are positioned as both biological and symbolic reproducers of the nation, they are also, in Anne McClintock's words, "denied any direct relation to national agency".[19] In the royal yearbooks and anniversary publications, it is clear that the female body is constantly used as a vehicle to reproduce the nation and nationalist conceptions and ideas. Pregnancy and childbirth are written into a discourse where royal children are born for the sake of kingdom and country. The female body giving royal birth gives rise to feelings of national affinity and kinship. The institution of monarchy is thereby tied to a strong sense of national community: "the whole country rejoiced". The female body enables the reproduction of the nation as well as of the institution of monarchy; it is clearly positioned at the centre of nationalist discourse.

Sexuality and Visual Desire

While the king as head of state symbolizes the Swedish nation, I argue that the female body, pregnancy and childbirth are essential if the monarch is to successfully symbolize and embody the nation. The relation between the king, the Swedish national community, and the queen, takes the form of a sort of double identification: "his" queen is also "our" queen. This identification between the present king and a national "we" is clearly manifested when the royal marriage is described. "The time was 12:21 and it was Saturday 19 June 1976 when the young king got a wife and the country a queen".[20] Here king and country are interchangeable – they are both getting married. A sense of national participation in the wedding ceremony itself is created: "we" were there and "we" can remember: "Saturday 19 June will remain hidden in our hearts as a glimmering happy memory."[21]

Important events in the life of the monarch are also constructed as important events for the national community. What has happened to the king has also happened to "us". The wedding, consequently, is described as a historical moment not just for the two people actually getting married, but also for the nation: "And certainly she was lovely, Silvia Renate, the chosen one. When she walked up the aisle of Storkyrkan together with King Carl Gustaf, she also walked straight into Swedish history."[22] However, for the bride, admittance to "Swedish history" is conditioned not only by being selected by the king, but also by being approved of by the people. The king's choice of spouse is confirmed and legitimated by a national "we": "Wherever she travelled she was met by spontaneous tributes and generosity from people who had sensed the future queen's human capacity." Gaining the approval of the people is connected to a visual display of her body. The king "shows her" to the photographers. For the first time, she "presented herself to the Swedish people as a Swedish citizen".[23] It is essential that she *appears* before the people: her body displayed and evaluated.

On the Saturday, the day after the announcement of the engagement, the couple came forward and appeared before the people. It is certainly no exaggeration to claim that Silvia Renate charmed the entire Swedish population. She is stunningly beautiful, has a disarming smile and is quite certainly the most beautiful queen on the Swedish throne.[24]

As the people approve of the king's choice of wife, a popular partaking of his love affair begins. The people are described as a sort of third party in the relationship. "Hands were raised throughout the crowd, people wanted to touch the woman who had given new life to the Swedish crown, a human being of flesh and blood, a young queen by the king's side."[25] The sentiments and emotionality displayed in the yearbooks are striking. It is as if not only the king, but the entire Swedish population is falling deeper and deeper in love with the future queen. Her physical assets are constantly pointed out: "the girl with the long black hair and the warm smile".[26] Details concerning her constitution and capabilities are lamented on. She is a couple of centimetres taller than her future husband, and she can play the accordion. She has a strong character and is cheerful, while also being restrained and self-possessed.[27] As the day of the wedding approaches, the people get to know the bride better and better: "During Silvia's wanderings through Stockholm the Swedish people could see for themselves that she was not at all as tall as previously had been said. Actually Silvia was a few centimetres shorter than the king."[28]

This popular participation in the king's love affair and marriage involves the future queen being seen as desirable not only in relation to her husband, but in relation also to a national "we". That he desires her – and finds her desirable – is matched by the national "we" being seen as having a collective desire to *see* her. And as she is depicted as beautiful, as stunningly beautiful, this collective desire is also fulfilled: "The cheering burst forth and rose towards the summer sky, flags waved and the packed crowd rejoiced. All over Old Town people were hanging out of the windows. Everyone wanted to see the Most Beautiful Queen on the Swedish Throne."[29]

In the yearbooks and jubilee publications, the public is depicted as having a longing to look, a sort of visual desire, in relation to the queen, but also in relation to the other female members and in particular in relation to the children of the royal family: "most people want to take a really good look at the royal children". [30] The annual official photo-sessions are long awaited. The world has "been waiting for these photographs", photographs that allow the Swedish people to "reunite with their crown princess".[31] Similarly, the clothes and coiffures worn on formal occasions are claimed to be a matter of "curiosity, inspection and admiration".[32] The fact that this desire – this longing to gaze upon – actually is fulfilled is apparent in the yearbooks. Fulfilment is closely tied to the proclaimed beauty and charm of the royal females. Victoria is, as one yearbook claims, "sweet, suntanned and natural. Just the way one wants one's crown princess."[33]

Body and Beauty

The desire to gaze upon the queen, as well as the satisfaction displayed as the object in question lives up to expectations of femininity, charm and beauty, is explicit in the yearbooks. The queen's body is described as something to be visually experienced and enjoyed: "The TV-viewers [...] could enjoy the sight of Queen Silvia conversing with her partner".[34] She is quite simply "an eyeful".[35] The yearbooks contain an excessive number of statements dwelling on the beauty of the queen, describing her as dazzling, a fairy queen, constantly catching everyone's eye and everywhere an object of incessant admiration.[36]

Here, the female body is given meaning as pure flesh, an object to be looked upon. This can be understood in terms of how vision, seeing and being seen, has been interwoven with gender relations. "[A] man can always be seen. Women are looked at", states Susan Sontag.[37] And John Berger describes a similar thought:

> [M]en act and women appear. Men look at women. Women watch themselves being looked at. This determines not only most relations between men and women but also the relation of women to themselves. The surveyor of woman in herself is male: the surveyed female. Thus she turns herself into an object of vision: a sight.[38]

In the royal yearbooks, the female body comes across as something to be visually experienced, a sort of treat for the eyes. "No assignment is more rewarding than photographing Queen Silvia, and no more unrewarding than explaining that she is even more beautiful in real life", explicates one yearbook. [39] And under the heading "Queen Silvia's many faces", another yearbook publishes twelve portraits of the queen. In the short text that accompanies this collage

Visual desire. Reprint from *Det lyckliga året* (1978). *Photo:* Jessica Lund/National Library of Sweden.

of pictures, the desire to look as well as the satisfaction of having this desire fulfilled is apparent:

> Wherever Queen Silvia appears she stirs up great and justified attention. Always in suitable creations and hats, when the setting so demands. Queen Silvia does not hesitate to broaden her wardrobe and readily tries on new combinations. Here we have collected twelve pictures from the happy year, pictures that display everyday life as well as more festive occasions. But of course it is not all about clothes – Queen Silvia is also a living human being who always has a smile on hand. A warm glimmer in her eyes, a smile, sweet laughter. Maybe that is why she is so loved.[40]

The detailed accounts of clothes and hair, of dresses, hats and jewellery underline how the female body is groomed, adorned and dressed up in order to come across as a genuinely special and remarkable object. Objectification is so encompassing that, as in the quote above, it has to be pointed out that we are dealing with a real person. These descriptions of dress and appearance show how the enjoyment invested in gazing upon the royal female body is also tied to the objectification mediated by pictures and text. A national "we" is seeing a sight. Together "we" experience a desirable object.

In numerous ways, the yearbooks and anniversary publications construct the female body as a desirable object. The smallest details of clothes, hair and jewellery are dwelled upon. The gala dresses in particular are described in an elaborate way.[41] Adorned in the glittering gold of the crown jewels, the female body is turned into a site where national history and lineage is spelled out. The jewels of the Swedish kingdom adorn her body, jewels that kings now dead have commissioned, collected and passed on. Heritage, monarchy and conceptions of the nation are here intertwined and acted out on the royal female body. Her body is put at the disposal of the nation. This process is evident also with regard to state visits. Officially the king alone represents Sweden. However, the queen's body, her looks, her hair, hats, beauty and clothes are invested with meaning on these occasions.[42] The queen's proclaimed beauty is linked to national pride: "we" should be happy that "we" have such a beautiful queen.

Numerous feminist researchers have pointed out the fact that women are burdened with representing and living up to national ideas and identity.[43] Women's bodies and appearances tend to be used and positioned as usable, for numerous kinds of nationalistic projects: giving birth, being displayed, being used to honour foreign heads of state. Having your self and subjectivity reduced to body and flesh is tantamount to not being an active subject, in possession of your own self.[44] A queen is quite simply there for "us"; she is there for "us" to enjoy. "We were lucky", writes one yearbook, "not only King Carl Gustaf can congratulate himself on such a charming wife. The kingdom of Sweden can also congratulate itself on having a queen who represents her country so well."[45]

National Pleasure

Through the analysis of the yearbooks and anniversary publications, I have tried to elucidate how gender and nation are constantly intertwined and how gender relations and nationalism confirm and reinforce each other. The female body makes possible the reproduction of monarchy, and through childbirth the royal family is closely tied to feelings of national community and fellowship. The desire to gaze upon the royal female body – and the satisfaction that accompanies this gazing – is nationally coded. It is a visual desire that is both structured by and reinforces fundamental conceptions of gender, sexuality and nation. The construction of a national "we" that wants to lay eyes upon royal females and children legitimizes both constitutional monarchy as a form of government and the Swedish nation as the self-evident political community. By portraying the female body as beautiful and desirable, the visual craving in itself is legitimized and can also be unproblematically satisfied. After all, who does not want to look at a beautiful woman?

In feminist theory, it is often underlined that the female body has been positioned as a symbol of the national community. The processes I have tried to explicate here, however, adhere to a somewhat different logic. The Swedish king embodies and symbolizes the Swedish nation – he is interchangeable with a national "we". Nevertheless, the queen has been the focus of a collective desire. National community is negotiated not through male desire for an abstract or symbolic female figure that embodies the nation, but rather through participation in male desire for a beautiful and desirable woman. The position of the queen is consequently not that of embodying or symbolizing the nation. Her position is rather one of legitimizing and confirming the heterosexuality and virility of her husband as well as of the national community.

The present analysis of the royal yearbooks and anniversary publications makes explicit that constitutional monarchy as a form of government – with its linkages to reproduction, bloodlines and heritage – also entails naturalization of gender relations and of the nation. Monarchy naturalizes established conceptions of nation, history, gender, heterosexuality and body while, simultaneously, these conceptions naturalize monarchy. A nationalistic and hetero-normative political community is thereby negotiated. Albeit banal, the royal yearbooks mediate royal life and the monarchy in itself as extraordinary and spectacular. I would argue that a key feature of the central role of the monarchy in the reproduction of Swedish national identity and community can rightly be found in this seductive mix of the ordinary and the extraordinary, of the banal and the spectacular.

On one level, the royal yearbooks and jubilee publications simply tell a story of everyday human existence, the passing of life: of birthdays, childbirths, vacations, family anniversaries, ageing and death. When these events of everyday life involve members of the royal family, however, the emotional and sentimental underpinnings of national identity are supported by the fact that a personal identification with the royal family appears as natural and self-evident.

"They" are people just like "us", they (also) get married and have children, their children grow up, and they grow old and die. The banality of the whole affair – that the royal family consists of ordinary people just like "us", and that what is acted out is "ordinary" life in an enlarged and spectacular version – makes possible this nationalistic and narcissistic emotionality.

Notes

1. This article – a revised version of "En nationell njutning: Kropp och kön i kungliga årsböcker", *Kvinnovetenskaplig tidskrift* 2006 (1) – is written as part of a research project entitled "Monarchy and Democracy in Sweden 1970-2000", funded by the Swedish Research Council (Vetenskapsrådet).
2. Orvar Löfgren, "Nationella arenor", in Billy Ehn et al. (eds), *Försvenskningen av Sverige: Det nationellas förvandlingar* (Stockholm: Natur & Kultur, 1993), and Ann Towns, "Paradoxes of (In)Equality: Something is Rotten in the Gender Equal State of Sweden", *Cooperation and Conflict* 2002 (2).
3. See, for example, Maud Eduards, *Kroppspolitik: Om Moder Svea och andra kvinnor* (Stockholm: Atlas Akademi, 2007), and Anne McClintock, *Imperial Leather: Race, Gender and Sexuality in the Imperial Contest* (New York & London: Routledge, 1995).
4. Nira Yuval-Davis, *Gender and Nation* (London: Sage, 1997).
5. Joan B. Landes, *Visualizing the Nation: Gender, Representation and Revolution in Eighteenth-Century France* (Ithaca & London: Cornell University Press, 2001).
6. Michael Billig, *Talking of the Royal Family* (London & New York: Routledge, 1992), p. 25.
7. Neil Blain & Hugh O'Donnell, *Media, Monarchy, and Power* (Bristol: Intellect, 2003), p. 43.
8. Michael Billig, *Banal Nationalism* (London: Sage, 1995).
9. A number of royal yearbooks have been published in Sweden on an annual basis. Special jubilee publications are furthermore published in connection with royal birthdays, anniversaries and other kinds of festive occasions. The present article is based on editions of yearbooks and anniversary publications issued between 1973 and 2000. The material analysed includes *Vårt kungapar* (*Our Royal Couple*), published from 1976 by Semic, and a series of books written by journalist Bobby Andström and published 1975 by Williams förlag, from 1976 to 1986 by Askild & Kärnekull and from 1987, under the title of *Det kungliga året* (*The Royal Year*), by Natur & Kultur, as well as a number of occasional jubilee and anniversary publications, among these the lavish publication produced by Bonniers publishers in connection with the present king's 50th birthday, *Femtio år med kungen: från lillprins till monark* (*Fifty Years with the King: From Little Prince to Monarch*), written by Björn Viberg (Stockholm: Albert Bonniers förlag, 1996).
10. Successionsordning 1810:0926, reprint SFS 1979:935.The constitution is written in a way that links monarchy to the descendants of Carl XVI Gustaf. If no heirs are available, the constitution will have to be rewritten. Since 1980, no distinction is made between female and male descendants. The right of succession is restricted to children born in wedlock.
11. *Femtio år med kungen: Från lillprins till monark*, p. 8.
12. *Vårt kungapar: Året som gått med den kungliga familjen*, 2, *Ett år med drottning Silvia*, Caj Andersson & Gisela Andersson (eds) (Sundbyberg: Semic, 1977), p. 36, *Vårt kungapar: Året som gått med den kungliga familjen*, 8, *Tio år med kungen*, Agneta Hyllén & Barbro Scherrer (eds) (Sundbyberg: Semic, 1983), p. 46.
13. *Vårt kungapar: Året som gått med den kungliga familjen*, 20, *Kronprinsessan Victoria 18 år*, Barbro Scherrer (ed) (Sundbyberg: Semic, 1995), p. 54.
14. *Vårt kungapar* 1977, p. 54.
15. *Vårt kungapar: Året som gått med den kungliga familjen*, 3, *Den lyckliga familjen*, Caj Andersson & Gisela Andersson (eds) (Sundbyberg: Semic, 1978), p. 3.

16. Billig analyses the gender-dynamics surrounding female monarchs in *Talking of the Royal Family*, pp. 173-175, compare Julie Burchill, *Diana* (Stockholm: Feminista, 2003). On the historical positioning of Swedish female monarchs in relation to discourses on motherhood and reproduction, see Malin Grundberg, *Ceremoniernas makt: Maktöverföring och genus i Vasatidens kungliga ceremonier* (Lund: Nordic Academic Press, 2005), Karin Tegenborg Falkdalen, *Kungen är en kvinna: Retorik och praktik kring kvinnliga monarker under tidigmodern tid* (Umeå: Department of Historical Studies, 2003) and Charlotte Tornbjer, *Den nationella modern: Moderskap i konstruktioner av nationell svensk gemenskap under 1900-talets första hälft* (Lund: Department of History, 2002).

17. One line of argumentation in the parliamentary debate on equal right to succession for male and female children was that if this reform were put into action, the throne would pass on to a new dynasty as a crown princess got married, Riksdagens protokoll 1977/78:125, 20/4 1978.

18. *Vårt kungapar* 1995, p. 65.

19. McClintock, *Imperial Leather*, p. 354; compare Julie Mostov, "Sexing the Nation/Desexing the Body: Politics of National Identity in Former Yugoslavia", in Tamar Mayer (ed), *Gender Ironies of Nationalism: Sexing the Nation* (London & New York: Routledge, 2000).

20. *Vårt kungapar: Året som gått med den kungliga familjen*, 1, *Carl Gustaf och Silvia*, Caj Andersson & Gisela Andersson (eds) (Sundbyberg: Semic, 1976), p. 49, *Femtio år med kungen: Från lillprins till monark*, p. 86.

21. Bobby Andström, *Silvia och kungen* (Stockholm: Askild & Kärnekull, 1976), p. 51, *Vårt kungapar* 1976, p. 64.

22. *Silvia och kungen*, p. 9.

23. *Vårt kungapar* 1976, p. 29, 1983, p. 10.

24. *Silvia och kungen*, p. 79.

25. Bobby Andström, *Drottning Silvias första år* (Stockholm: Askild & Kärnekull, 1977), p. 17.

26. *Silvia och kungen*, p. 63.

27. *Vårt kungapar* 1976, p. 20.

28. Ibid p. 32.

29. *Silvia och kungen*, p. 33.

30. Clas Göran Carlsson, *Året med kungafamiljen* (Höganäs: Wiken, 1984), p. 95. The public is also ascribed a wish to see the king. A wish that also is fulfilled when, for example, the king waves to the people from the royal balcony on his birthday. The wish to lay eyes upon the king differs qualitatively, I would argue, from the desire to see the queen. It is not the king's body or physique that is visually interesting, but rather his symbolical status and social position.

31. *Vårt kungapar: Året som gått med den kungliga familjen*, 4, *Kungafamiljen i fest och vardag*, Caj Andersson & Gisela Andersson (eds) (Sundbyberg: Semic, 1979), p. 2; *Vårt kungapar: Året som gått med den kungliga familjen*, 23, Barbro Scherrer (ed) (Sundbyberg: Semic, 1998), p. 50.

32. *Vårt kungapar: Året som gått med den kungliga familjen*, 16, Barbro Scherrer (ed) (Sundbyberg: Semic, 1991), p. 12.

33. *Vårt kungapar: Året som gått med den kungliga familjen*, 24, Barbro Scherrer (ed) (Sundbyberg: Semic, 1999), p. 62.

34. *Vårt kungapar* 1983, p. 71.

35. *Vårt kungapar: Året som gått med den kungliga familjen*, 15, Barbro Scherrer (ed) (Sundbyberg: Semic, 1990), p. 58.

36. Bobby Andström, *Det kungliga året* (Stockholm: Natur & Kultur, 1991), p. 9, 1992, p. 11, 1998, p. 37, 2001 p. 1; *Vårt kungapar* 1983, p. 69; *Vårt kungapar: Året som gått med den kungliga familjen*, 13; *Kunglig vardag och fest*, Barbro Scherrer (ed) (Sundbyberg: Semic, 1988), p. 7; *Vårt kungapar: Året som gått med den kungliga familjen*, 21, *Carl XVI Gustaf 50 år*, Barbro Scherrer (ed) (Sundbyberg: Semic, 1996), p. 13.

37. Susan Sontag, "Women", in Anne Leibovitz & Susan Sontag, *Women* (New York: Random House, 1999), p. 23.

38. John Berger, *Ways of Seeing* (London: BBC & Penguin Books, 1972), p. 47.
39. *Året med kungafamiljen* 1984, p. 51.
40. Bobby Andström, *Det lyckliga året* (Stockholm: Askild & Kärnekull, 1978), p. 58.
41. See, for example, *Vårt kungapar* 1979, p. 50, 1983, p. 5, 1996, p. 13; *Det lyckliga året* 1978, p. 44.
42. *Det lyckliga året* 1978, p. 44; *Vårt kungapar: Året som gått med den kungliga familjen*, 5, *Ett år tillsammans,* Caj Andersson & Gisela Andersson (eds) (Sundbyberg: Semic, 1980), p. 40.
43. For an overview of this literature, see Maria Jansson, Maria Wendt & Cecilia Åse, "Kön och nation i vardag och vetenskap", *Statsvetenskaplig tidskrift* 2007 (3).
44. Cecilia Åse, *Makten att se: Om kropp och kvinnlighet i lagens namn* (Malmö: Liber, 2000), pp. 101-102; compare Dorothy E. Smith, *Texts, Facts and Femininity: Exploring the Relations of Ruling* (London: Routledge, 1990), pp. 191–192.
45. *Vårt kungapar* 1991, p. 64.

The Royal Napkin

Sanctifying Processes in the Media Landscape

Mattias Frihammar

Behind locked doors, in a safe cupboard deep in the archive of the Royal Armoury in Stockholm, rests article number 33020. It is not an ancient fragile object, or a valuable piece of art, or a golden crown, but a simple, not to say banal thing. Article number 33020 is a plain, ordinary cotton napkin, cut in pieces, just a few years old.

It took this napkin eight months in 2003 to change from an anonymous part of a table setting into an isolated and preserved part of the royal Swedish heritage. In the present article, I analyse this transformative progression, paying special attention to the part media played in the process. This is a story of how mass-media attention accumulates further media attention, and (in this case) contributes to the concept of heritage, and it is a story of how social stratification and hierarchy organizing take place in an apparently emancipated context. Last but not least, it is a story of how royal charisma is produced by activities fully in accordance with late-modern irony and rationality.[1]

The basic premise of the analysis is a constructivist one, in the sense that I understand the massive royal visibility in the media to be a component in the construction of royalty, rather than a consequence of royalty itself. More explicitly, in the present analysis, I do not consider "royalty" to be something with a fixed content of meaning, but rather a phenomenon that constantly produces and re-produces itself.[2] The story of a napkin becoming royal is a good example of this theoretical point of view. The napkin in itself is a very mundane item and the royalty of the napkin has been assembled without any strategic involvement from the royal court or the royalties. King Carl XVI Gustaf appears as the catalyst in this process, yet the actions that charged the napkin with royalty are out of the hands of the royal institution. Royalty is at the centre of this story, but actual royalties and their actions play but a minor role.

Royal Events as Media Tradition

The napkin now resting in the archive of the Royal Armoury was once part of the table setting at the Sports Gala, an annual live broadcast television event, where the most successful athletes of the year are celebrated. The gala performance took place at the Stockholm Globe Arenas, 20 January 2003, with live music, prize-giving and entertainment in front of a big dining audience. The king was an honorary guest.

During the evening, comedians Robert Gustafsson and Henrik Schyffert, well known to the Swedish audience, appeared in sketches.[3] In one sketch they acted as antagonistic party planners who eventually start to argue and chase each other among the audience. Gustafsson ran away from Schyffert and got a grip on the king's chair. When Schyffert threw a paper towel at Gustafsson, the latter loudly proclaimed "You can't touch me while I'm holding the king". The audience burst into laughter. The king, captured as he was by the TV cameras, played along. He laughed and took his napkin and placed it on his head to protect himself from the childish party planner behind him. This initiative made the audience laugh even more and the king was applauded for his gesture. As the king put the napkin on his head, Gustafsson reached out and touched the king's head with his hands.[4]

As Head of State, the king's personal lifecycle also concerns the nation; royal anniversaries, weddings and funerals are broadcast as precious moments purportedly belonging to the nation as a whole.[5] Due to this recursive appearance, TV programmes about royalties obtain a recognizable form in their own right, and royalty appears in a more or less traditionalized form.[6] In this context, it has been argued that it is fruitful to analyse traditionalized performances as following a manuscript.[7] This "manuscript of tradition" is to be understood as a manuscript in motion, constantly rewritten, and hardly noticed. The point is that the manuscript gives the participants a cultural framework by which they can understand an event as a meaningful occasion. Over the years, comedian Robert Gustafsson has often appeared as an entertainer at broadcast royal occasions, where his performances include irreverent interaction with royalties and other celebrities.[8] If we think of broadcast royal events as following a manuscript of tradition, Gustafsson takes the role of a kind of modern day court jester, creating a form of domesticated and expected mockery of royalty. The joke with the king at the gala performance may appear to be somewhat blasphemous when considered as an isolated event. But following a manuscript of tradition, it is an expected performance that confirms royal authority, rather than objecting to it.[9]

The broadcast Sports Gala is the first time the napkin appears in media. It comes into view in the periphery, not at all on display as a valuable or special item. In this part of the process, the napkin is part of the frame; it does not stand out or draw attention to itself. At the same time it takes a key position, in its own humble way. As Daniel Miller points out, scholars of culture have to draw attention to the fact that "objects are important not because they are evident and physically constrain or enable, but often precisely because we do not 'see' them".[10] In this case, the napkin on the king's head becomes a significant detail, a materialized acceptance that establishes a playful frame of meaning, a royal white flag expressing agreement and permission to play and laugh. The napkin is a secure membrane between Robert Gustafsson and the royal body, allowing Gustafsson to lay his hands on the royal head, without the risk of violating the royal noble distance.

News-Bill Logic

The next day, the incident is on the news bill for one of the two major evening papers. It is referred to as a "Coup against the king during the television gala", and there is also a picture of the incident, the king with the napkin on his head and Robert Gustafsson behind him with his hands on the king's head. It almost looks as if Gustafsson is blessing the king with his hands, in the way historic kings, by virtue of their divine authority, blessed their subjects.

A news-bill's message exaggerating the contours of the event it refers to. *Photo:* Mattias Frihammar.

The incident is now becoming a media event in a literal sense of the word: one kind of media puts an episode, which was arranged and performed in another media form, on further display.[11] One obvious explanation of the news bill is that royalty sells. However, let us look further into this logic, both generally and specifically, and see whether we can detect some other meanings.

A news bill is a tool for an evening newspaper to attract buyers. It is an advertisement or an informational tool designed to raise the interest of potential readers about the content of the newspaper. A newspaper is a journalistic product and as such one of its main tasks is to produce and provide news. This makes the news bill a marketing tool for news. An event presented as news has to be unexpected, but at the same time it has to be referred to in a way that confirms the knowledge and expectations of the receiver. This is what Stuart Hall talks about as the paradox of news making.[12] And if this is true of news in general, then the news bill is a medium that stresses this paradox even further. The news bill comprises only a few words that are to make the receiver recognise both the event and the unexpected dimension of it.

Royalty is well suited to news bills because there is little need for contextualization. By using one word, *king*, the news bill refers to a well-known person whom everybody immediately relates to as a particular character and has an opinion about.

In this particular case, the news bill refers to an incident on a television programme, which many readers have probably seen for themselves. The "news" then, in reality, becomes the fact that what happened should be considered "a coup". It is not a coup d'état, or a coup against the official role of the king, but rather a coup that can be understood in intimate terms. The logic presupposes personal identification with the person Carl Gustaf, who suddenly becomes the centre of attention. In this way, the news bill confirms the concept of the king both as an ordinary man (who gets embarrassed when exposed to unexpected attention) and as an extraordinary being (whose embarrassment demands media attention).[13] The reporting becomes part of the soap-opera style of reporting the life of royalty, which constantly takes place in the tabloid press, and which stresses personal identification with royalty, alongside submissive admiration.

This story could have ended here. The napkin has had its 15 minutes of fame. It had been the news headline of the day, and could now have fallen back into the sheltered life of anonymity. But royalty attracts media in a particular way, and in this story the media become self-supporting.

Modern Irony

Soon after the incident and the news bill, radio journalist Kjell Eriksson, who at the time had a radio show, "Lie-in", on the youth-oriented national channel P3, announced that he had attended the Sports Gala, and that, when all the guests had left, he had stolen "the king's napkin". For a few days the napkin became a regular conversational feature in his show; the napkin, listeners were informed, was kept in a plastic bag from Konsum (an established Swedish cooperative supermarket chain), which he always carried with him.

The spectacle put on display in the programme is performed by the journalist himself, Kjell Eriksson, and the napkin takes on the role of bearer of royalty in a more explicit way than before. The napkin gets its own link on the website of the programme. The story is presented as follows:

It was the Sports Gala in 2003. The Globe was filled with sport stars, royalties and by Kjell. And the king stood up after dinner and disappeared with his followers. Kjell was thrown around in the crowded place, and suddenly happened to stand beside the king's chair.

– Did the king really sit here? Kjell asked a waiter who was clearing the table.

– Yes, the king sat here, he answered.

And there it was. The king's napkin.

And then...

Praise the Lord, here is the tax refund! To take from the rich and give to the poor! Now is the time for the roasted sparrows to bring joy and happiness, now is the time for the people to get their share, a cheerful Kjell burst out after the Sports Gala.[14]

There is an obvious ironic tone in the description, which corresponds to the general satirical tone of the programme. We understand that Eriksson does not really consider the napkin to be "a tax refund", and that it will not make "roasted sparrows bring joy and happiness".[15] By the apparently overstated enthusiasm expressed in the programme, we also understand that Ericsson does not really consider the napkin worthy of this attention.

Irony has a tendency to blow up, reduce and disfigure its subjects, working as a kind of semantic distorting mirror, which (if we understand it) makes us laugh. This could lead to the conclusion that the use of irony renders a message less sincere or important than if the message had been performed in a serious mode, as if the use of irony establishes a kind of moral reserve. But because being ironic is seemingly joining in on an argument that relates to you in some way (otherwise the topic would not be worth the attention), an ironic modus confirms the importance of the subject.

The irony in the radio programme follows a logic similar to that in the famous fairy tale "The Emperor's New Clothes" by H.C. Andersen; the emperor is naked but everybody acts as if he is wearing the most wonderful clothes, although in this story it is an ordinary napkin that makes everybody act as if it were extraordinary. But there is a significant difference: the radio-show listeners play the double role of the collaborative listeners to, and the silly subjects of, the joke. The programme addresses a modern self-assured person, who is aware of the distance between a media image and an authentic character. As David Chaney writes, present-day audiences are "aware of being manipulated through spectacle but accept it as a distinct form of public life and entertainment".[16] In this case, people laugh at the fact that they, as listeners, pay attention to a story about a napkin just because it has been touched by the king. They are seemingly equal to the journalist, his playmates rather than victims of the joke.

It is important to keep in mind that the ironic modus does not just dethrone the royal sovereignty. For example, Eriksson lets us know that he carries the napkin in a plastic bag from the cooperative supermarket chain Konsum. The cooperative movement in Sweden is associated with egalitarian ideals and should be considered an anti-monarchist movement. Choosing to put the napkin in the Konsum bag could thus be seen as an act of irreverence, a way of expressing a republican attitude. But the ironic context does something else:

instead of questioning the reason for a monarchic form of government, the ironic framework transforms the irreverent action into a joke, and as such, a domesticated action that confirms, rather than questions, a royal mandate.

As modernity is always struggling with the task of how to maintain the vision of society, reality and ourselves as uniform, rational and coherent entities, the royal status causes problems.[17] How can one acknowledge the evident differences between a royalty and an average person, without violating principles of egalitarianism and equality? Irony steps in as one of modernity's strategies for dealing with these contradictory sentiments, as a way to establish a coherent sphere in an inconsistent reality. The ironic discussion about the royal napkin on the radio programme and on the website places the discussion about royalty in a reflective discourse, which allows comments in a wider sense of (assumed) common ideas about royalty and the monarchy. The ironic idiom makes it possible to simultaneously take on the role of a devoted and ingenuous victim of royal gravity as well as the role of a rational modern individual who sees through the royal illusion.

The Napkin as a Prize and the Price of the Napkin

According to Kjell Eriksson, the napkin attracts all sorts of people. Many listeners want to have the napkin, and they write e-mails to him asking for it. Eriksson also tells the audience that a reporter from a national news programme visited the studio only to put the napkin on his head just as the king had done. Due to this apparent widespread desire for the napkin, Eriksson decides to arrange a quiz so that listeners can call the programme and answer questions about the royal family. If they give the right answer, they can win a numbered and framed piece of the "royal" napkin, under the slogan "Take from the rich, give to the poor".

As part of the preparations for the quiz, well-known antiques expert Knut Knutson, from the popular Swedish version of the television show "Antiques Roadshow", visited the programme and evaluated the napkin. He dismissed the intrinsic quality of the napkin as worthless, saying that it is machine made and lacks patina, but he evaluated the napkin as being worth a "couple of thousand Swedish kronor" on a charity auction, owing to the fact that it had once belonged to the king.[18] Knutson cut out the first piece of the napkin, and the quiz could start.

One of the qualities of royalty, which it shares with art, is that it goes beyond economic estimation, it is said to have an affectionate value, which cannot be translated into a monetary value. As we live in a world of merchandise where almost all things around us are primarily evaluated as products on a market, objects that are understood as valuable, in non-economic terms, have to fight hard to avoid devaluation.

Pierre Bourdieu has shown how firm denial of economic significance, by the right people in the art world, is the main condition for high economic value

A framed piece of the napkin at the Royal Armoury's storehouse. *Photo:* Mattias Frihammar.

when a work of art is evaluated on the open market.[19] Bourdieu borrows the concept of consecration from the religious context, where consecration is an act performed by priests to separate a thing from a common and profane use to a sacred use. To make use of Bourdieu's concept of consecration in our story, we can say that the napkin is consecrated by the actions of Knutson. Knutson challenges the ironic and distanced way of approaching the napkin because he is a recognized authority in the field of valuation, and a celebrity in his own right. He is a legitimate priest who is able to recognize authenticity in a temple of superficial goods, and when Knutson states that the napkin is worthless in itself, he is also implying a non-worldly value that derives from the connection with the king. The relevance of Knutson's consecration is threefold: first, Knutson himself makes a conspicuous imprint on the napkin by making the first cut, bringing the napkin some of the patina he said it lacked; second, an expert proves that the kingly touch can introduce royalty into an ordinary object; and third, there is rational confirmation that the napkin is worth money on the open market.

Humorous Liturgy and Substantial Consequences

During the same period as the quiz show was broadcast, the Royal Armoury was preparing for the exhibition "Gustav Vasa Revisited: Swedes' Royal Mementoes". This was an exhibition that displayed royal artefacts that ordinary people had at home. The curator Ann Grönhammar, who had heard about the royal quiz, contacted Kjell Eriksson and asked him if he would be willing to donate the remains of the napkin to the exhibition, which he was.

This gave Eriksson an opportunity to entertain further, and he arranged for a live broadcast of the ceremonial handing over of the napkin to the director of the museum, outside the museum in the Royal Palace. While a wind ensemble played, Eriksson made a speech as the napkin lay on a pillow. At the end of the speech, Eriksson asked: "Do you, director of the museum Barbro Bursell, take this treasure back, to nurse and to take care of until retirement do you part?" And, of course, Bursell said: "Yes!"[20] To reconcile the act, the ensemble played a fanfare, and to acknowledge the new status of the napkin as part of the royal Swedish heritage, the museum officials taking care of the napkin put on their white gloves.

There are many layers in this ceremony. The first apparent layer is a radio show, dressed up as a humorous ritual, borrowing components from ceremonies such as marriages and inaugurations, playing and entertaining with conventions and expectations. Second, it is a seriously exercised donation procedure, in which the museum authority incorporates the napkin into the museum collection. Third, the ceremony, as it appears on radio, is a pedagogic display and examination in real time of the concept of heritage, inviting an attentive listener to reflect on what heritage is and how and why it is manifested. It is a humorous liturgy that has substantial consequences.

When the exhibition opened, the napkin was the first object presented to the visitors, with a text that explained its history from the Sports Gala to the handing over ceremony. As a medium, a museum exercises authority in a very confident way, with a strict body of regulations and a convincing scientific connotation. The museum asserts itself as a secure authority of authenticity, carefully documenting the provenance of the things collected. Regarding provenance, the napkin seems to be a perfect example, because the media have documented the whole process. The fact that Eriksson could be regarded as a weak link – how do we really know that he, a known satirist, did not simply take any napkin just for fun? – is effectively neglected in the confirming

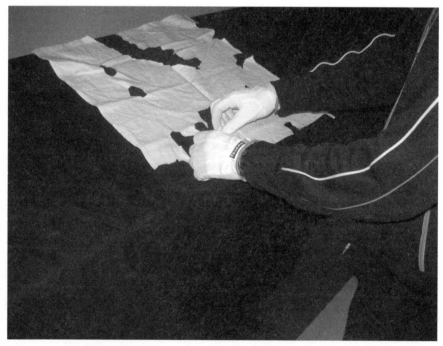

Item number 33020 of the Royal Armoury. *Photo:* Mattias Frihammar.

context of the museum. When the exhibition was over, the napkin was put in the archive, and is kept there under the description "Napkin used by Carl XVI Gustaf at the Swedish Sports Gala at the Globe Arenas 20 January 2003. [---] Cut in pieces, originally square napkin in white cotton? (sic) The cloth is creased and has many holes."

Conclusion

This is the story of how an ordinary cotton napkin has made a transformative journey, and how it, through transactions of value, has made its way into the archive of the Royal Armoury as part of the royal Swedish heritage. The media have played an important role in this process. The incident that at first distinguished the napkin from other napkins was arranged and performed in a television programme, and this incident was in turn brought to general attention by an evening paper. A radio show then made use of the attention the incident already had, by putting a napkin on further display, claiming it was the napkin that had been seen on the king's head. This caused the Royal Armoury to open its eyes to the napkin as an item of national interest. Without all this media attention, there would not have been any story to tell, but the more media limelight the napkin got, the more it seemed to shine with a royal glance.

Neither members of the royal family nor of the court actively participated in the transformative process in which the napkin became royal. The king put the napkin on his head, but it appeared to be a spontaneous act. This indicates that the definition of what it means to become royal is, at least in part, out of the hands of the royalties. In a news era of mass culture, it is hard for public figures to control their medial appearances and that apparently applies to the apex of the social hierarchy as well, the royal family.[21] In a way, they can be regarded more as "public figures" than "royalties".[22]

Considering the way in which this extraordinary royal status is assembled in this story, the approach to the napkin gradually becomes more serious: starting with the obvious joke at the Sports Gala, where the napkin is part of the frame that does not draw attention, moving on to the news bill, where the napkin was to be seen in the exposed contact point between the comedian and the king. In the radio show, a more ironic attitude is adopted towards the napkin; its simplicity as well as its connection to the king is stressed. With Knut Knutson's cheerful, but nonetheless professional evaluation, the approach becomes more serious, and at the end, when the museum takes over, the museum officials take a sympathetic, yet solemn approach.

The approach becomes increasingly serious, but nowhere in the process is the tone noticeably reverent. The extraordinary facet of royalty is perceived in different practices, but never in respectful rhetoric. It is the attention as such that makes royalty the social summit, not reverent words or austere gestures.

Notes

1. The analysis of the napkin's metamorphosis is part of my current doctoral research in ethnology on contemporary royalty in Sweden. The bulk of the fieldwork is centred on royal municipal visits. My focus is on the social performances that generate the royal status, where I am more concerned with the actions and strategies of "ordinary people" than with those of the royal family and the court.

2. This does not mean that we as individuals or groups can make whatever we want of any given category, for example, royalty. All categories are imbedded in varyingly powerful and far-reaching networks of meanings and artefacts, symbols, laws, traditions, understandings and so on, and the possibilities to make changes or make things different are fundamentally unevenly distributed. The core of the statement is that categories, for example royalty, cannot be anything other than what we make of them.

3. Both Gustafsson and Schyffert are well-established entertainers and actors in a satiric and ironic humour tradition. They have, together and individually, appeared in numerous programmes, films and shows since the early 1990s, many of them considered national ground-breaking classics in the satiric and humoristic genre.

4. The episode can be seen on YouTube: http://www.youtube.com/watch?v=uwtTP5G4c0A (25 June 2008).

5. According to David Chaney, "The Mediated Monarchy", in David Morley & Kevin Robins (eds), *British Cultural Studies: Geography, Nationality, and Identity* (Oxford: Oxford University Press 2001), p. 207, royalty has "come to constitute one of the more significant televisual genres". But even everyday unpretentious occurrences are reported on as being of importance to the nation as a whole. Cecilia Åse, in her contribution to this book, shows how exposure of royal everyday life reproduces national coded feelings of participation, loyalties, compassion and joy.

6. This does not mean that the viewers regard such programmes as a tradition, but rather that when they see them they are familiar with the narrative form and components.

7. Lotten Gustafsson [Reinius], "Bocken brinner! En dialog på offentlig plats och i Gävles lokalpress", in Barbro Klein (ed), *Gatan är vår! Ritualer på offentliga platser* (Stockholm: Carlssons, 1995), p. 199.

8. See for example Gustafsson's speech at the king's 50th anniversary http://www.youtube.com/watch?v=yxp-wW73v2Q (25 June 2008).

9. Louise Phillips, "Media Discourse and the Danish Monarchy: Reconciling Egalitarianism and Royalism", *Media, Culture & Society* 1999 (21), p. 221, pinpoints a similar circumstance in an analysis of media coverage of the wedding between the younger son of the queen of Denmark, Prince Joachim to Alexandra Manley in 1995. Phillips argues that apparently mocking initiatives (for example an incident in which a newspaper arranged for a, at the time well-known gatecrasher, Monsieur Claude, to enter the event uninvited) uphold royalist rather than republican meanings, but refers to a "discourse of royalty that contains elements of egalitarianism", rather than to a manuscript of tradition.

10. Daniel Miller, "Materiality: An Introduction", in Daniel Miller (ed), *Materiality* (Durham, N.C.: Duke University Press, 2005), p. 5.

11. Media event is a concept that is understood differently by professional journalists and within media studies, anthropology and ethnology. In journalistic jargon, a media event is a negative concept which implies that a scene has been staged to facilitate (or govern) the job of the journalist, and thus is a less authentic reporting scene, while Daniel Dayan and Elihu Katz introduced the concept media event to describe how big public events such as state funerals, sporting games and, especially interesting for this anthology, royal weddings are arranged directly to suite the television medium as such, thereby becoming more of a ritual, which for example connects centre and periphery and confirms prevailing social structures, than an instance of news reporting. See Karin Becker, "Medierna och de rituella processerna", in Barbro Klein (ed); see also Daniel Dayan & Elihu Katz, *Media Events: The Live Broadcasting of History*. (Cambridge Mass.: Harvard University Press, 1992).

12. Stuart Hall, "The Determination of News Photographs", in Stanley Cohen & Jock Young (eds), *The Manufacture of News: Social Problems, Deviance and the Mass Media* (London: Constable, 1973).

13. It is, however, likely that the king, or at least the royal court, is aware of and has accepted the joke to come. I have not examined this, as it is not a crucial point here. The image conveyed, both in the television programme and in the newspaper, is that of an unprepared king.

14. http://www.sr.se/p3/Sovmorgon/kungen.stm (25 June 2008).

15. By using the formulation "Praise the Lord, here is the tax refund", the presentation alludes to an episode in the Disney cartoon version of the story of Robin Hood, annually broadcasted at Christmas Eve, and by using the metaphor "roasted sparrows" it is satirically alluding to a criticized metaphor from the king's Christmas speech in 2002.

16. Chaney, p. 215.

17. Slavoj Žižek, *The Sublime Object of Ideology* (London: Verso, 1989).

18. The evaluation can be heard on http://www.sr.se/p3/sovmorgon/kungen.stm (25 June 2008). 1,000 Swedish kronor is equivalent to approximately 100 euro.

19. Pierre Bourdieu "The Production of Belief", *Media, Culture & Society,* 1980 (2), pp. 61–93.

20. From Kjell Eriksson's manuscript in The Royal Armoury.

21. Chaney, p. 211.

22. Phillips, p. 227, draws a similar conclusion, writing: "The construction of images of royalty does not only depend on actual behaviour of the royal family but on the policy of the media vis-à-vis coverage of the private lives of the monarchy."

A King without E-mail

Reflections on New Media and the Royal Court

Pelle Snickars

In mid-June 1996, the Swedish royal court went virtual. Prior analogue information strategies had been deemed old fashioned, and it was time for something new – the Internet. During the mid-1990s, the World Wide Web communication protocol transferring information on the Internet had become increasingly popular. Sun Microsystems launched the slogan "The Network is the Computer", and in 1994, the new Web browser Netscape Navigator was released. By 1996, almost 80 per cent of people surfing the Web used the Navigator browser. So did the Swedish court, and the Royal Information and Press Department – hereafter the Press Department – bought a Web domain: www.kungahuset.se. The court was thus digitally upgraded and soon the royal family was online with a dedicated homepage. Because of the great interest from English-speaking countries, half a year later the three sub-sites "The Monarchy in Sweden", "The Royal Family" and "The Royal Palace" were also released in English versions at royalcourt.se. Of these, "The Royal Family" attracted most attention. Complete with colour portraits, the king, the queen and the crown princess were presented with biographical details. The entire Bernadotte Dynasty was even displayed in the form of a graphical family tree. However, visitors seeking to get in touch with the court must surely have been disappointed, as the site specifically stressed in bold letters: "We would like to point out that His Majesty the King of Sweden does not have an e-mail address."[1]

No e-mail. For most of us today this sounds like an anomaly. But the Internet in 1996 was poles apart from today's multilayered Web of converging media forms. Not only has the Web witnessed the fall of Netscape Navigator, and its subsequent replacement by Microsoft's Internet Explorer as the default Web browser, but the World Wide Web has also gone through numerous changes and lately even been socially upgraded to the so-called Web 2.0. According to Tim O'Reilly, Web 2.0 is "the business revolution in the computer industry caused by the move to the Internet as platform, and an attempt to understand the rules for success on that new platform. Chief among those rules is this: build applications that harness network effects [which get] better the more people use them."[2] The upgrading of the Web can also be described as a shift from websites with static information to new sites working more as interlinked, dynamic computing platforms. Contemporary visitors at the sophisticated and elaborate royalcourt.se can, for example, go to the media centre and experience the court in moving images; they can read all official press releases, listen to the king's speeches and browse through the royal diary.

With applications such as Wikipedia, Facebook, MySpace and blogs, the "do-it-yourself" revolution of the Web is, indeed, a fact. In a Swedish context, Bengt Wahlström has argued that four new scenes or arenas constitute the basis of the virtual society: blogs, social networking sites such as Facebook – as well as sites with media like YouTube – virtual worlds such as Second Life, and collaborative systems like Wikipedia. Wahlström claims that these arenas have an increased influence in areas of society such as politics, culture and trade – "power 2.0" in his terminology.[3] As a new asset, Web 2.0 is fundamentally bottom-up driven; it is the people using software and creating content who are in charge. This, however, has led to a number of dilemmas. The act of publishing, for instance, has more or less ceased to exist as a semantic concept, as there are basically no gatekeepers within the digital domain. Anyone can "publish" a blog on anything, and there is a risk that critical examination will be neglected. Then again, blogs and user-generated content are regularly distributed for free or under a creative commons license. Besides, content is often uploaded to social networking sites with characteristics different from those of traditional media such as newspapers, radio or television.

Given the rapid and converging changes in the contemporary media landscape, the purpose of the present article is to reflect on the role of new media and Web 2.0 in relation to the Swedish royal family, as well as to present a sketchy survey of more or less controversial instances involving the court and new media.

Mediated Proximity

Traditionally, the media have been important for the court; being visible in mediated form has after all been almost an imperative for a king. In addition, there is – and has been – a tremendous public interest in the royal family. In 2003 alone, more than 7,000 articles appeared in the press dealing with the Swedish court.[4] Today, that very same interest has also gone online. On YouTube there are hundreds of clips with reference to the Swedish royal family, and recently Swedish Television (SVT) launched a specific sub-site devoted entirely to the court – "Kungahuset". However, the mediated symbiosis between the royal family and mainstream media has also been challenged by user-generated content on the Web as well as by the court's own usage of digital technologies, notably their recently upgraded Web page. Apparently, King Carl XVI Gustaf takes an interest in development of the homepage, and even "chatting with the king" has been on the agenda.[5]

During the summer of 2007, a profile of the king appeared on the social networking site Facebook. "Carl XVI Gustaf", it seemed, had already gathered a few friends and supposedly started the group "We who rule Sweden". The profile, however, turned out to be a fake, and in August, the tabloid *Aftonbladet* reported that "a Web fraudster had stolen the king's identity".[6] As it turned out, the Swedish king was in good company; the prime minister also had a fake profile as well as Mona Sahlin, the leader of the Social Democratic Party. In fact, when reporters checked the site more carefully, they discovered that Princess Madeleine had several fake profiles on Facebook. The director of the Press Department, Nina Eldh, was very upset and promised to take action to eliminate these profiles. The event sparked frequent comments within the blogosphere.

Ultimately, the various royal profiles were removed. A year later, however, the king is now back on Facebook, boasting more than 300 friends. The old profile "Carl XVI Gustaf" has been reinstated with the new profile "Kung Carl Gustaf".

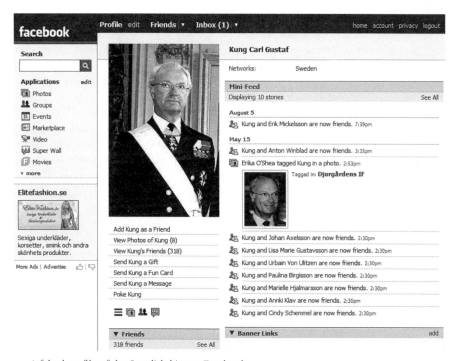

A faked profile of the Swedish king at Facebook.

The Web, of course, promises a mediated proximity, and social media depend on interactions between people using technology as a conduit. In fact, Facebook recently became the most popular global social networking site; as of June 2008, Facebook had 132 million unique visitors, thereby dethroning

MySpace.[7] The site facilitates "being friends" with people, and there is also a possibility to effortlessly approach celebrities as well as to get in contact with former friends using applications such as "discover people you may know". Networks of friends' networks, then, generate an almost infinite range of potential contacts.

Even so, the "Kung Carl Gustaf" profile is quite obviously a fake. Apart from photographs of the king himself, ads for female underwear and site-generated comments, so-called mini-feeds (for example, "Kung and Lisa are now friends"), reveal the profile as a fraud. Then again, the Press Department has lately received e-mails on a regular basis asking whether the king actually is present on Facebook.[8] One of the complicated things about social media is, thus, the underlying uncertainty as to whether or not information is reliable. Without editorial control, basically anything goes. However, Wikipedia has also proven that "false articles" are re-edited – sometimes within minutes of their appearance.[9] Still, critique of the social Web concerning its trustworthiness and reliability is significant; it remains an important issue that one should not too easily brush away.[10]

Stealing someone's identity on the Web is, of course, a little too wicked and malicious. However, the existence of a fake king also generates questions regarding the lack of a royal presence in various social networking communities. If the court is having problems with fake royal identities, why not simply create a few official profiles? Using Facebook is easy, and the Press Department could quickly have fashioned a profile and demonstrated royal progressiveness with regard to Web 2.0. The Swedish Institute, for example, has revealed the numerous political and public advantages of being present online. The head of the institute, Olle Wästberg, has claimed that the 400,000 Swedish kronor spent on the Second House of Sweden in Second Life is one of his greatest investments. During the inauguration of the virtual embassy in May 2007, Wästberg stated that it "is a real pleasure to see that so much media, above all the foreign press, has recognized how progressive Sweden is. The great interest that this has generated in the media is estimated to have already paid off tenfold."[11]

The royal court, however, has confirmed their seeming lack of interest in the social Web. On a query from *Aftonbladet*, as to whether the king had any plans of creating his own Facebook profile – let alone a blog, Nina Eldh answered that she did not think this would interest him.[12] This has left the digital field open, so to speak, and the court has had to cope with various more or less unpleasant incidents. At a number of occasions, the royal family has been offended by what they regard as media infringements; intrusions that arguably have become more common with the arrival of the Internet and the Web. On the photo-sharing site Flickr.com, for example, a search for "Crown Princess Victoria" generates 184 hits with pictures of her taken by various people. These are all unofficial photographs of a royal celebrity, images totally beyond the control of the court. At present, however, most of them are nice and agreeable. One example among many is the signature Snow Kisses Sky – a Chinese male living in Yunnan – who in December 2005 took a fine portrait of Princess Victoria at the Swedish embassy in Beijing.

"HRH Crown Princess Victoria
of Sweden. Photo taken in
Royal Swedish Embassy in
China." Uploaded to Flickr by
Snow Kisses Sky in December
2005.

Tagging it with keywords such as "princess", "celebrity", "Victoria", "Swedish", "Scandinavian" etcetera, this image has as of August 2008 been viewed 1,653 times, and most comments on the photo are positive: "Wow. I love your portraits"; "What shot you made there :)" or "Great photo! She is so beautiful!" In the comments list, the photographer himself has also stated that "it was a rare opportunity for me to meet such a celebrity. My colleagues were interviewing with her [sic] when I took this shot."[13]

The policy of Flickr and the community guidelines stipulate that "if you are offended by a photo or video you can either click away or you can mark it as poorly moderated by clicking on the 'Flag this photo' link. [...] If you think there's immediate cause for concern, you can report content and/or someone's behaviour to Flickr staff via the 'Report Abuse' link."[14] In other words, there is an editorial staff in place to prevent various infringements. However, there is no Flickr policy for someone who wants a "normal" image of him- or herself to be deleted. The obvious lack of control over images is actually a defining characteristic of the social Web. User-generated content – often uploaded anonymously as with the signature Snow Kisses Sky – makes it hard to criticize and reprove accusations in visual or textual form. Articles appearing on Web blogs – the glossy tabloid *Svensk Damtidning*, for example, has no less than three "royal blogs" with all the latest gossip surrounding the court – are dynamic, active and constantly up to date. Texts can be transformed, altered and changed, and the same applies to videos. *Svensk Damtidning* also has a Web-TV application with numerous short video clips showing the court, in general, and the royal children as well as events with royal presence, in particular.

One could argue that in the case of a controversy surrounding the court, more articles or videos rather than apologies will in all likelihood appear on the Web, not least because the blogosphere is full of both anti-royalist writers and celebrity spotting aficionados. In some ways, then, new digital media function differently from traditional media. New media have, for instance, replaced the "one-to-many" broadcasting model of traditional communication with the possibility of Web-based "many-to-many" communication. In fact, the very foundation of Web 2.0 is based on the latter model – or more precisely on "many-to-few" communication. Web pages, blogs, file sharing and social networking sites are media forms that function according to a logic whereby information and announcements are communicated by numerous people, but often only noticed by a few. However, new media are also distinguished by interactivity and their networkable nature, and owing to their binary character they are regularly described as manipulable. In relation to the Swedish court, the latter is certainly the case as evidenced by the many forged images circulating on the Web. Common retouching and editing of royal photographs, in fact, caused numerous readers to mistakenly believe that images published in the press of Princess Madeleine after the Nobel celebrations in 2002 were digitally manipulated because of her low-cut décolletage.[15]

Generally speaking, it is, thus, fair to state that through digital upgrading, royal media coverage has become more intrusive than before. This, in turn, has led to a number of controversies. Most of them are related to paparazzi-like methods, yet some also have a more critical posture. In October 2002, Queen Silvia, for example, was interviewed in the public service programme "Pippirull" – a radio programme that has been available online ever since. Polite as always, she answered questions concerning the condition of elderly care in Sweden. The interview, however, was filled with references and allusions to Nazism, concentration camps and gas chambers, implicitly referring to the fact that the queen's father, Walther Sommerlath, became a member of the German National Socialist Party already in 1934.

The king allegedly found the interview "distasteful".[16] Nonetheless, it was thought of as satirical and humorous by the originators, alluding to the fact that neither the queen nor the mainstream media have really dealt with the compromising past of the Sommerlath family.[17] In the annual report from the court, however, the radio programme was referred to as "the macabre interview with the queen." It is said to have been one of three media events during the year in which the Press Department had to deal with countless questions from the public.[18] As polls often indicate that 70 to 80 per cent of the Swedish population have positive attitudes towards monarchy as a system of government, most enquiries expressed support for the queen.[19] In fact, making fun of the court is often double edged. In terms of satire, there remains a division among Swedes who, on the one hand, regard the royal court as sort of a ridiculous antique institution, and Swedes who, on the other hand, see the royal family as part of Sweden's true cultural heritage. As a consequence, mainstream media often display a servile and fawning manner when interviewing the court. This is most apparent in the yearly SVT programme on the royal family, usually screened at prime time during the Christmas holidays. The producer Inger Milldén at SVT has stated that, "the programme we are making upholds a tradition; it follows the royal family during the year. It is not a critical or an examining programme, and neither is it produced by that type of journalists."[20]

One might argue that the servile manner of journalists has to do in part with the personal distance kept by the court. No one is allowed to come close, and therefore somewhat paradoxically, the critical questions never seem to be asked. In January 2008, the SVT programme "Debatt" actually discussed the very issue of journalists fawning on the court. A number of reporters were critical of how the media approached and described the royal family, and the programme host, Stina Dabrowski, had invited the king himself to give his opinion. The court's Press Department initially approved of the programme. They did want someone from the court to take part. Carl XVI Gustaf, however, put in his veto and, basically, prohibited anyone from participating. As a consequence, Dabrowski – a TV personality with a long career – went public during the programme with these quite extraordinary circumstances. The Press Department, then, suddenly backed the king, and in an interview in *Expressen* the day after an offended Dabrowski claimed: "I sometimes get the impression that [the court] does not want to have ordinary journalism near the royal family. As soon as [the Press Department] suspects something that resembles such reporting, it tries to keep them away."[21]

One of the more interesting opinions expressed in the TV programme "Debatt" came from Annette Kullenberg. She claimed that journalists working for tabloids or the gutter press often acted and performed in a similar way as the court itself did. Journalists too, are dependent on the symbiosis between media and monarchy, and have to follow the rules of the game; that is, they need their job, and their job is to fawn on the court.[22] A case in point during spring 2008, more or less proving Kullenberg's claim, has been the TV programme about the fiancé of Crown Princess Victoria, Daniel Westling, entitled "His Royal Highness Westling". Originally scheduled to be broadcast in mid-April, the programme was removed from the TV tableaux due to uncertainties about the archival material used. According to an article in the trade journal *Resumé*, the Head of SVT's event department, Kerstin Danielsson, had stopped the film by maintaining rights to archival footage that SVT could not use without permission from the court. Furthermore, and citing an anonymous source, *Resumé* claimed that the event department "more or less acted as the court's branch at SVT; responsible for a great many interferences in programmes or features with the royal family. All programmes produced by the event department are [therefore] obedient and submissive."[23] As is mentioned in the introduction to this book, "His Royal Highness Westling" was finally screened in June 2008. However, the court then complained about and objected to the title; officially Daniel Westling was not (yet) part of the court, and hence not dignified as a royal member.

This etiquette in many ways goes hand in hand with the media's servile attitude towards the court, but class and good manners also matter. The royal family belongs to the upper class, and their private friends fit into a similar stratum of society. Aware of their privileged situation, the upper class, in fact, rarely express what could be regarded as politically incorrect opinions in front of cameras or microphones.[24] Traditionally, the media have thus had a deep respect for the royal family's status and privacy, probably linked to the general public support of the monarchy. After all, it was during the Olympics in Athens 2004 that a Swedish reporter for the very first time – instead of using the appropriate "Your Majesty" – dared to address the king in the second person singular. In various interviews, one can often notice a detachment or lack of involvement from the royals, which regarding the king also has to do with his official and apolitical role. He is, basically, prohibited from having an opinion, and hence in the media comes across to viewers or listeners as somewhat disinterested.

In light of the above, the 1996 Web declaration that "His Majesty the King of Sweden does not have an e-mail address" seems quite appropriate. Interviews and contact with the media are necessary, but the king apparently desires to limit communication to traditional channels. In contrast, Swedish politicians have, certainly, been more willing to accept new media in their occupation. Sweden's Foreign Minister Carl Bildt, for example, has had a blog for more than three years. In fact, already in 1994 he began sending out a weekly e-mail to an interested public. This was two years prior to the court's announcement that it was not possible to get in contact with the king through new communications technologies. As a result, the court ignored new ways of communicating with admirers and royal enthusiasts. One might think, however, that the situation today would have changed, considering the court's new elaborate Webpage. However, the same inability to get in touch remains. The king still does not have an e-mail address – at least not an official one. Somewhat amusingly, it is stated that one "should write a letter to the Royal Court", if one would truly like to receive a personal reaction from the king.[25] Thus, it seems that in the digital world, analogue communication is a way to keep a traditional distance as well as to filter unwanted messages.

Soft Power

In a time of networked and personified communication, the inability to send the king a simple e-mail seems quite atypical and, frankly, uncharacteristic of the court. Historically, the royal family has always been user-friendly towards new media technologies. The nation's first and oldest X-ray image – dedicated to King Oscar II in 1898 – resides, for example, in the Bernadotte library. And Swedish film history even starts with him at the Stockholm exhibition in 1897.

Prior to being filmed, Oscar II is furthermore said to have been mesmerized by Edison's phonograph, and his funeral in 1908 was intensively mediated. The same year, the whole court, in all some 25 persons, gathered at the Stockholm Castle for a private screening on the 26th birthday of Crown Princess Margareta.[26] A similar approval and awareness of the media characterized the reign of King Gustavus V. And even if he initially objected to the radio broadcast of Princess Astrid's wedding in 1926, the king from then on became quite fond of the new broadcast medium. From the Stockholm Castle – he never cared to go to the studio of Swedish Radio downtown – he was a regular radio speaker to the whole nation during the 1930s, and especially throughout the Second World War.

Thus, if the royal family by tradition has been a rather conservative ideological bastion, it has developed a truly modern approach to the mass media. The current King Carl XVI Gustaf is, of course, well aware of the great public interest surrounding him and his family.

Ever since his marriage in 1976 – a televised event with some 400 million European viewers[27] – he has, for instance, had press assistant Elisabeth Tarras-Wahlberg at his side taking care of the media. By the time she left the court in 2004 – an event that in itself made the news – she had built up an impressive public relations machinery. As a spokeswoman for the court, in general, and the

Approximately 400 million viewers watched the Swedish royal wedding in 1976. Cover of *Röster i Radio-TV* 1976 (26).

king, in particular, Tarras-Wahlberg controlled the image of the royal family for almost 30 years. She has often been controversial, but apparently quite skilled. Today she often lectures on how to handle the media.[28] Moreover, in interviews conducted after she left the court, she has stated that during the past decade it has been her duty to teach the royal children how to deal with the media. They have lately been the prime targets of particularly the tabloids. Browsing through the court's annual reports, one easily finds evidence of intense media coverage – which has sometimes prompted the court to take legal action. In 2003, for example, a number of German tabloids – with a regular interest in the Swedish court – insinuated that the royal couple's marriage was coming to an end. Together with digitally manipulated images and a photo montage, speculations were made as to whether a divorce was to be filed. Because these accusations were false, the court sued some of the tabloids, which were consequently later forced to publish apologies.

Apparently the court receives more than a hundred requests every month regarding various events that people, organizations or companies want the king or the royal couple to inaugurate or otherwise be part of. Carl XVI Gustaf's main occupation is, actually, taking part in such events. During 2007 alone, he participated in almost 150 gatherings. Various forms of media coverage make him an attractive figure, and companies are, naturally, keen to engage him, because their chances of getting media attention increase tenfold. Thus, even if the king has an official and apolitical role, the Swedish monarchy is certainly an institution with influence on many levels. For example, Carl XVI Gustaf's very personal speech in January 2005, shortly after the tsunami catastrophe, in which he explicitly referred to his own loss of his father – who died in a plane crash in 1947 when the king was an infant – was publicly appreciated as words of comfort. The primary reason was the expression of personal and private mourning from an otherwise somewhat reserved king. Thus, at least to some extent, the royal family makes use of what Joseph Nye has called "soft power". Nye's notion refers to the media's ability to politically influence people through conceptions, thought patterns and mediated ideals. In order to establish positive attitudes, Nye has argued that various mass media content is almost as important as how a country's domestic and foreign politics are being run.[29]

The notion of mediated soft power in relation to the court is, however, more constructive when describing the Swedish royal family's relation to media prior to 1950. It is important to remember that King Gustavus VI Adolphus – who in October 1950 succeeded Gustavus V – actually was the first Swedish king without any formal political power whatsoever. Gustavus V, however, deliberately used media in various political ways. Film cameras, press reporters and radio microphones constantly followed him; Swedish Film Industry alone depicted him on more than 500 occasions. This symbiotic relation seems to have created an insight into the power of especially visual media. In fact, already around 1900, members of the Swedish royal court – for example Prince Wilhelm, later a devoted filmmaker – understood and became conscious of the power of the media and the desirability of offering their mediated image to ensure popularity and position. Of Sweden's ten oldest surviving films, nine depict monarchs and members of royal families.

These films, as well as innumerable features in the press, suggest that the decrease in actual royal power during the first part of the twentieth century due to parliamentary democracy stands in direct proportion to the increase in royal exposure in contemporary mass media. The same argument has been made by Franziska Windt in a book on the mediation of Wilhelmine Germany. Wilhelm II, for example, is sometimes described as Germany's first film star, and countless actuality films depict him, not to mention the innumerable photographs – a "Majestätische Bilderflut" – with hundreds of thousands of coloured reproductions of him.[30] The potential of modern media was obvious to various courts, and the mass culture of modernity identified as a source of soft power. Using media became a way to implement political and social influence. Just as public persons today know the value and advantages of media coverage, monarchs of the past would permit press photographers, phonographic and film companies to attend various events, because they knew the importance of being documented and mass produced in image, sound and film.

Hence, the symbiotic and "soft power" relation of media exposure so apparent today with regard to celebrities and public persons in fact developed during the first decades of the twentieth century. Media representatives would predominantly use royal fame to increase commercial popularity, and the courts took advantage of the public attention caused by the mediation. Obviously, this symbiosis had a precursor in royal courts' relations to artists and painters. However, the difference with regard to modern mass media was the public scale, dimension and range of the royal mediation. A royal portrait in an art gallery around 1750 might have been seen by a thousand people. In comparison, millions of people saw royal films in cinemas.

Moreover, the courts' modern management of and attitude towards public relations stand in sharp contrast to parties and politicians who (apart from in the US) saw film, for example, as lowbrow and cheap entertainment. Compared with conditions today, where politicians have been keen to use new media, we see an inverted relation to media participation. In the past, the press was of course important for political parties, but other media were often deemed politically uninteresting. The Social Democrats in Sweden, for example, despised the new medium of film – even though cinema audiences were dominated by the working classes. Up until the mid-1930s, the Swedish labour movement was, actually, more hostile towards the different mass media of modernity than was the bourgeoisie or the aristocracy. A true paradox, indeed, because most of the movement's prominent representatives like Hjalmar Branting and Per Albin Hansson initially worked with media as newspaper editors.[31]

Today the situation is different; while the Social Democrats are present on YouTube, the royal court tries to ward off social media with aloofness and seeming disinterest. In response to a direct question put forward to the Press Department as to whether the court had any plans of using new media apart from the Web, the answer was negative.[32] However, one reason might be that the Press Department itself has lately been the subject of an online media debate concerning whether it is using the right communication strategies in a new digital environment. For example, on several occasions during spring 2008, the trade journal *Dagens Media* published reports concerning the unease and discomfort caused by the new leadership of Nina Eldh. Six persons apparently left the Press Department during the spring, leaving only three persons to deal with media issues. At the same time, Eldh has also expressed concern about the decrease in royal publicity. Still, according to her, the Press Department "is not a campaign organization for the monarchy. It is a very special job, as it concerns the Head of the State and his family. Basically, it is our task to inform about the daily work of the king and the queen."[33]

"Kungahuset" & YouTube

On Sweden's national day, 6 June 2008, Swedish public service television launched a sub-site entirely devoted to the royal family – "Kungahuset". The purpose of the site is to offer viewers old archival material related to the court, as well as current reports on the royal family's activities and whereabouts. Of course, SVT's idea is to draw on the popularity of the court to generate user clicks on the company's Webpage. A few days prior to the Web launch, the afore-mentioned TV programme, "His Royal Highness Westling", was finally screened. Yet TV critics expressed reluctance and hesitation regarding SVT's new royal media strategy. Some were exceedingly critical describing, for example, the Web launch as totally bizarre.[34] Yet as Bertil Mollberger in *Dagens Nyheter* stated: "it is a sign of the times. The film [on Westling] would have been unthinkable in public service the decade after 1968. Now, however, the swing of the pendulum is a fact, and our TV sets display one royal report after the other."[35]

SVT's site "Kungahuset" is, however, interesting, because it utilizes the TV archive as a digital source of content. The first film displayed in the list of the video application SVT Play under the heading "Kungahuset" is, for example, Prince Wilhelm's short documentary *About a Naval City* (1937), a film about the city Karlskrona and its shipping legacy.

Just underneath in the list, one finds an archival portrait focusing on King Gustavus VI Adolphus, *The King in Close-Up* (1962).[36] None of these films, how-ever, are listed with their correct title – an apparent consequence of archival negligence. On the Web, however, these films are re-used as archival content. The Internet as well as the Web is in fact gradually changing the very forms of media in an archival direction. An archival mode of online media is evident both in new forms of television and radio – "More than 2,000 hours of free TV: whenever you like!" is, for example, the logo for SVT Play – as well as in the enormous media clusters shared in the P2P networks.

Sites such as SVT's "Kungahuset" are, thus, changing or altering media forms in archival directions, and one of the explicit visions for "Kungahuset" was actually to upgrade archival content into digital formats. "This is an idea we

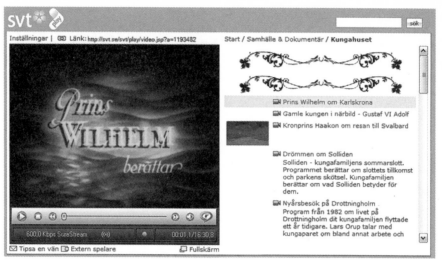

Prince Wilhelm remediated at SVT's website "Kungahuset" in the summer of 2008.

have had for quite some time", Eva Landahl from SVT stated in an interview. "We have tremendous amounts of [royal] material since way back in time. The idea is to make a site like 'Öppet arkiv' but more topically oriented."[37] The open archive, referred to in the quotation, has been SVT's platform for archival online material since March 2005, and "Kungahuset" in many ways resembles the strategies deployed by the former site. However, the purpose of "Kunga-huset" is also to upload new content to the video blog "Kungahusbloggen". In mid-July 2008, for example, a short video clip from Crown Princess Victoria's birthday celebrations was added to the royal video blog. The three-minute clip looks almost like amateur footage; there is no voice-over commentary and the camera zooms rapidly in and out. Only towards the end of the clip, with a number of images of the audience, does one get the feeling that this is a professional feature.

According to Wikipedia, a "blog" – a contraction of "Web log" – is a site "with regular entries of commentary, descriptions of events, or other material such as graphics or video. [...] Many blogs provide commentary or news on a particular subject; others function as more personal online diaries. A typical blog combines text, images, and links to other blogs".[38] Thus, if a video blog such as "Kungahusbloggen" is to remain true to its kind, entries do have to follow the established aesthetics of that specific media form. However, publishing amateurish footage on the national public service broadcaster's Webpage is somewhat odd. Naturally, people at SVT know how to make TV programmes. Consequently, the idea behind the royal video blog remains peculiar, not least because some material is obviously re-runs of former televised features.

One way to grasp and comprehend SVT's royal blog strategy is to connect it to current developments in the contemporary audiovisual media landscape, notably YouTube. Regular news on svt.se, for example, has moved from a programme structure to a clip format. The latest news attraction online, Play Rapport, is a specific application with a long list of short audiovisual news items. The programme structure is defined by the user, and SVT's blended media strategy also allows users to copy content to their blog, while still being in control of the code. This means that whenever someone looks at a SVT clip from any blog whatsoever, the SVT click frequency increases. As Martin Jönsson has stated in a blog entry on Play Rapport, the new SVT media strategy is quite astonishing.[39] Only two years ago, SVT threatened to sue YouTube for copyright infringement. Now they have their own channel on YouTube with more than 250 clips, and in addition their media material is spread out through the blogosphere. Public service is, thus, being distributed in completely new ways.

Despite everything, the driving force behind current changes in audiovisual media distribution is naturally YouTube. Only three years after its foundation in 2005, YouTube has become the very epitome of digital culture. Seemingly outpacing cinema and television in terms of popularity, this brand-name video distribution platform promises endless new opportunities for amateur video and political material, as well as entertainment formats and viral marketing. Attracting a global mainstream audience and activating users to form communities and share audiovisual material, YouTube likewise seems to redefine moving images, audiences and producers. What this actually implies is a question currently pervading industry boardrooms, university classrooms and popular culture alike.

Numerous videos including the Swedish royal family have been uploaded on YouTube. Some of them are made by users themselves, and some consist of archival material that has been illegally posted. A four-minute video about the royal family preparing for Christmas during the 1980s quite obviously derives from SVT. The signature Ducinek, in addition, runs the YouTube community "Royalty forever" with numerous videos of European princesses and princes. Most of them are structured as a photo montage with added music. The video "Princess Madeleine 'Pretty Woman'", for instance – viewed 46,254 times – consists of hundreds of images of Princess Madeleine accompanied by a soundtrack of Roy Orbison's hit single. Other films look more like traditional so called "mash-up-videos", films that use low-resolution video material gathered from various online sources without any considerations of copyright whatsoever. Furthermore, 21 videos on YouTube have been tagged with "kungafamiljen" ("the royal family"), and among them are a number of sketches from the TV4 production "Hey Baberiba", a show with regular comic imitations of the royal family.

One interesting aspect of YouTube, related to the way videos tend to circulate on the Web, is the statistics and data flap available for all videos next to the commentary field. The video "Princess Madeleine 'Pretty Woman'", for example, is linked to five different URLs.[40] One of them is a Danish tabloid's Webpage, where the video has been seen almost 200 times. Audiovisual media, thus, tend to circulate more and more in similar ways as photography has done on the Web for quiet some time. The video "Princess Madeleine at Charlotte Kreuger's wedding" can be found on YouTube, as well as on the Web-TV application at svenskdamtidning.se. In fact, together with *Svenska Damtidning* the latter has even developed a "Swedish Royal Channel" on YouTube.[41]

"The Swedish Royal Channel" on YouTube in the summer of 2008.

The channel has had almost 2,500 views, yet only 37 people are active subscribers. In comparison, the "Royal Channel" of the British monarchy on YouTube has 21,830 subscribers with almost 1.6 million channel views.[42] Still, as with the case of Play Rapport, the main purpose of establishing such channels is to use a blended distribution strategy that facilitates and simplifies the circulation of moving image content on the Web.

Conclusion

The "Swedish Royal Channel" on YouTube is one example of how new media are used in relation to the court. Media material produced for one specific site is circulated and re-used on other domains too. Basically, SVT's "Kungahuset" deploys the same strategy, albeit with their own archival material. The public impact, however, is almost negligible – not least if one compares with international examples. The most viewed clip on the British "Royal Channel", for example, has been seen almost one million times by YouTube users.[43]

Even if new media content has led to some controversies regarding the Swedish court, notably the faked royal profiles on Facebook, one of the conclusions of the present article is that the traditional media still cause most concern for the court. Media debates about the Swedish royal family during the past years have predominantly concerned features in mainstream media, such as public service TV and radio programmes. The main reason is, on the one hand, the continued mass effect of traditional media forms. The new media do not replace the old media; instead media forms exist in parallel as long as the commercial potential exists for the old media. Thus, even if Web-based television, for example, is increasingly popular, its viewing rates can scarcely be compared to traditional TV broadcast figures. On the other hand, the royal court's management of public relations still emphasizes public service, because there remains a possibility to control output. Anti-royalist blogs, however, are impossible to restrict or regulate.

As a consequence, the mediated symbiosis between the royal court and mainstream media is now being confronted by various new forms of user-generated content. Traditional broadcast media, however, belong to the twentieth century, and in due time they will be replaced by the Web's "masses of media". Blogs, Flickr, YouTube and Facebook are forerunners – with numerous amateur features on the royal family that are beyond the control of the court. However, because these features do not receive a great deal of public attention, the court does not really care about them – at least not at the moment. Because niche media (still) belong to the margin, this is also the reason why the royal family – apart from its homepage – has not been interested in participating more extensively on the social Web.

• • •

Just before finishing this text, the Royal Court announced on 24 February 2009 that Crown Princess Victoria and Daniel Westling were engaged. The marriage is set for the summer of 2010 and news of the engagement triggered numerous reports and commentary in traditional and new media. Interestingly, the announcement from the Court was made through a five-minute video, posted both on YouTube and on the website of the Court. Three days later, as these final lines are written, the video on YouTube has been seen by more than 200,000 people. Comments have been disabled for the video, since almost a thousand users have posted their opinions on the event. Thus, it seems as if the Swedish Court has finally realised how usage of new social media can be a way to reach and interact with a substantial audience, while at the same time remaining in charge of both the message and the medium.

Notes

1. The site kungahuset.se/royalcourt.se has been stored by the Internet Archive's application "Wayback Machine". See http://web.archive.org/web/19961114055950/www.royalcourt. se/eng/index.html (15 August 2008).

2. Tom O'Reilly, "Web 2.0 Compact Definition: Trying Again" – http://radar.oreilly.com/2006/12/ web-20-compact-definition-tryi.html (15 August 2008).

3. See, Bengt Wahlström, *Guide till det virtuella samhället* (Stockholm: SNS Förlag, 2007).

4. "Året 2003 Kungl. Hovstaterna verksamhetsberättelse", p. 7. All the court's annual reports from 2002 onwards are available for download at http://www.royalcourt.se/.

5. Telephone conversation with Ann-Christine Jernberg at the Royal Information and Press Department 11 August 2008.

6. Mattias Carlsson, "Falsk kung utlagd på Facebook", *Aftonbladet* 26 August 2007.

7. Adam Erlandsson, "Myspace – en nöjd tvåa" *Svenska Dagbladet* 26 August 2008.

8. Telephone conversation with Ann-Christine Jernberg 11 August 2008.

9. For a lengthy discussion on Wikipedia, see Clay Shirky, *Here Comes Everybody: The Power of Organizing without Organizations* (New York: Penguin Press, 2008), pp. 109-143.

10. See for instance, Andrew Keen, *The Cult of the Amateur: How Today's Internet Is Killing Our Culture* (New York: Doubleday, 2007).

11. Olle Wästberg is cited from the article, "Sweden inaugurates virtual embassy" – http://www.si.se/templates/CommonPage_____3365.aspx (15 August 2008).

12. Carlsson.

13. Snow Kisses Sky is cited from the comments list at http://www.flickr.com/photos/bmgallery/71712913/ (15 August 2008).

14. See, http://www.flickr.com/guidelines.gne (15 August 2008).

15. For a discussion, see Kerstin Nilsson, "Madeleine – hyllad för sin 'hylla'", *Aftonbladet* 12 December 2002.

16. Daniel Nyhlén, "Jag skall slå ner Palmlöf", *Aftonbladet* 26 October 2003.

17. See, for example, the interview with the "Pippirull" producer Olle Plamlöf in Elin Ekselius, "Ballaste killen i klassen", *Svenska Dagladet* 5 December 2004.

18. "Året 2002 Kungl. Hovstaterna verksamhetsberättelse", p. 17.

19. According to the recent SOM study 2008, the public's confidence in the court is, still, high. The study's so-called "confidence balance" can vary between +100 and –100. Hence, the court's +25 situate the royal family on the same level of confidence among the public as, for example, the banking system or the United Nations. For a discussion, see Sören Holmberg & Lennart Weibull (eds), *Skilda världar: Trettiåtta kapitel om politik, medier och samhälle* (Göteborg: SOM-institutet, 2008), pp. 41-45.

20. Inger Milldén is cited from Anna-Klara Bratt's & Mats Deland's article, "Pressens olidliga hovsamhet", in Eva-Lotta Hultén (ed), *För Sverige i tiden* (Stockholm: Atlas, 2003), p. 47. The article is also available on the Web – http://ceifo.soc.se/files/pressens.pdf (15 August 2008).

21. Dabrowski is cited from Anders Sandqvist's article, "Hämnades på kungen", *Expressen* 18 January 2008.

22. The journalist Annette Kullenberg expressed these opinions in the TV programme, "Debatt: Fjäsket för kungahuset", screened on 17 January 2008 in Swedish Television. For a discussion, see also Lena Andersson, "Inställsamt om kungahuset", *Svenska Dagbladet* 5 January 2008.

23. Leif Holmkvist, "Hovet i konflikt med SVT", *Resumé* 15 May 2008. The programme's Swedish name is "Ers kungliga höghet Westling".

24. For a discussion on the Swedish upper class, see Susanna Popova, *Överklass: En bok om klass och identitet* (Stockholm: Lind & Co., 2007).

25. See http://www.kungahuset.se/html (15 August 2008).

26. Cinema programme for the Edison-Biografen cited from, Erik Lindorm (ed), *Gustaf V och hans tid* (Stockholm: Wahlström & Widstrand, 1939), p. 11.

27. See, *Röster i Radio/TV* 1976 (26).

28. See, Ulrika Lundberg, "Han är mest allmänbildad i Sverige: Elisabeth Tarras-Wahlberg berättar om sina år med kungafamiljen", *Aftonbladet* 28 April 2006.

29. Joseph Nye, *Soft Power* (New York: PublicAffairs, 2004).

30. Franziska Windt et al. (eds), *Die Kaiser und die Macht der Medien* (Berlin: Jaron Verlag, 2005).

31. For a discussion on the topic, see Mats Jönsson & Pelle Snickars (eds), *Medier & politik: Om arbetarrörelsens mediestrategier under 1900-talet* (Stockholm: SLBA, 2007) pp. 13-47.

32. Telephone conversation with Ann-Christine Jernberg 11 August 2008.

33. See for example, Niclas Rislund, "Haveriet på hovet", *Dagens Media* 2008 (10), and Niclas Rislund, "Kaos på hovets presstjänst: Sex har slutat under våren", *Dagens Media* 24 June 2008 (Web version).

34. Andreas Gustavsson, "SVT startar sajt om kungahuset", *ETC* 9 June 2008.

35. Bertil Mollberger, "Folkets otåliga väntan", *Dagens Nyheter* 2 June 2008.

36. Swedish titles are *Kring en örlogsstad* and *Kungen i närbild*.

37. Eva Landahl is cited from Erik Esbjörnsson's article, "SVT startar kungasajt", *Resumé* 5 June 2008.

38. See the entry "blog" at Wikipedia – http://en.wikipedia.org/wiki/Blog (15 August 2008).

39. Martin Jönsson, "Public service flyttar till bloggosfären" 5 May 2008 – http://blogg.svd.se/reklamochmedier?id=7045 (15 August 2008).

40. As of 15 August 2008, the video was available at: http://www.youtube.com/watch?v=iNxi1U-_JGE&feature=related.

41. See, http://www.youtube.com/user/svenskdam (15 August 2008).

42. Statistics taken from http://www.youtube.com/theroyalchannel (15 August 2008).

43. The video is entitled, "The Christmas Broadcast, 1957", and can be found at: http://www.youtube.com/watch?v=mBRP-o6Q85s (15 August 2008).

References

Åhlander, Lars (ed), *Svensk filmografi, 2, 1920-1929* (Stockholm: Svenska filminstitutet, 1982).

Alm, Mikael, & Britt-Inger Johansson (eds), *Scripts of Kingship: Essays on Bernadotte and Dynastic Formations in an Age of Revolution* (Uppsala: Department of History, 2008).

Anderson, Benedict, *Imagined Communities: Reflections on the Origin and Spread of Nationalism* (London & New York: Verso, 1991).

Andersson, Aron, *Vadstena klosterkyrka, 2, Inredning* (Stockholm: Almqvist & Wiksell International, 1983).

Andersson, Lars, *Pilgrimsmärken och vallfart: Medeltida pilgrimskultur i Skandinavien* (Lund: Almqvist & Wiksell International, 1989).

Åse, Cecilia, *Makten att se: Om kropp och kvinnlighet i lagens namn* (Malmö: Liber, 2000).

Åse, Cecilia, "En nationell njutning: Kropp och kön i kungliga årsböcker", *Kvinnovetenskaplig tidskrift* 2006 (1).

Atkinson, David, & Denis Cosgrove, "Urban Rhetoric and Embodied Identities: City, Nation, and Empire at the Vittorio Emanuele II Monument in Rome, 1870-1945", *Annales of the Association of American Geographers* 1998 (1).

Becker, Karin, "Medierna och de rituella processerna", in Barbro Klein (ed), *Gatan är vår! Ritualer på offentliga platser* (Stockholm: Carlssons, 1995).

Bengtsson, Bengt, "Regionfilmen och konstruktionen av folkhemmet", in Mats Jönsson & Pelle Snickars (eds), *Medier och politik: Om arbetarrörelsens mediestrategier under 1900-talet* (Stockholm: SLBA, 2007).

Bennet, Robert, *Vadstena klosterkyrka, 3, Gravminnen* (Stockholm: Almqvist & Wiksell International, 1985).

Berger, John, *Ways of Seeing* (London: BBC & Penguin Books, 1972).

Berggren, Lars, *Giordano Bruno på Campo dei Fiori: Ett monumentprojekt i Rom 1876–1889* (Lund: Wallin & Dalholm, 1991).

Berglund, Louise, *Guds stat och maktens villkor: Politiska ideal i Vadstena kloster ca 1370–1470* (Uppsala: Uppsala University, 2003).

Billig, Michael, *Talking of the Royal Family* (London & New York: Routledge, 1992).

Billig, Michael, *Banal Nationalism* (London: Sage, 1995).

Blain, Neil, & Hugh O'Donell, *Media, Monarchy, and Power* (Bristol: Intellect, 2003).

Bourdieu, Pierre, "The Production of Belief", *Media, Culture & Society* 1980 (2).

Bradley Warren, Nancy, "Kings, Saints and Nuns: Gender, Religion and Authority in the Reign of Henry V", *Viator: Medieval and Renaissance Studies* 1999 (30).

Bratt, Anna-Klara, & Mats Deland, "Pressens olidliga hovsamhet", in Eva-Lotta Hultén (ed), *För Sverige i tiden* (Stockholm: Atlas, 2003).

Briggs, Asa, & Peter Burke, *A Social History of the Media: From Gutenberg to the Internet* (Cambridge: Polity Press, 2002).

Brooks, Chris, *The Albert Memorial: The Prince Consort National Memorial, Its History, Context, and Conversation* (New Haven: Yale University Press, 2000).

Burchill, Julie, *Diana* (Stockholm: Feminista, 2003).

Burke, Peter, *The Fabrication of Louis XIV* (New Haven: Yale University Press, 1992).

Cannadine, David, "The Context, Performance and Meaning of Ritual: The British Monarchy and 'The Invention of Tradition', c. 1820-1977", in Eric Hobsbawm & Terence Ranger (eds), *The Invention of Tradition* (Cambridge: Cambridge University Press, 1983).

Chaney, David, "The Mediated Monarchy", in David Morley & Kevin Robins (eds), *British Cultural Studies: Geography, Nationality, and Identity* (Oxford: Oxford University Press 2001).

Cnattingius, Hans, *Studies in the Order of St. Bridget of Sweden*, 1, *The Crisis in the 1420s* (Stockholm: Almqvist & Wiksell, 1963).

Connell, R.W., *Masculinities* (Cambridge: Polity Press, 1995).

Couldry, Nick, *Media Rituals: A Critical Approach* (London: Routledge, 2003).

Couldry, Nick, "Transvaluing Media Studies: Or, Beyond the Myth of the Mediated Centre", in James Curran & David Morley (eds), *Media and Cultural Theory* (London: Routledge, 2006).

Darnton, Robert, "An Early Information Society: News and Media in Eighteenth-Century Paris", *American Historical Review* 2000 (1).

Dayan, Daniel, & Elihu Katz, *Media Events: The Live Broadcasting of History* (Cambridge, Mass.: Harvard University Press, 1992).

Douglas, Mary, *How Institutions Think* (London: Routledge & Kegan Paul, 1987).

Duby, Georges, *The Three Orders* (Chicago: University of Chicago Press, 1980).

Duffy, Eamon, *The Stripping of the Altars: Traditional Religion in England 1400-1580* (New Haven & London: Yale University Press, 2005).

Eduards, Maud, *Kroppspolitik: Om Moder Svea och andra kvinnor* (Stockholm: Atlas Akademi, 2007).

Ekström, Anders, *Den utställda världen: Stockholmsutställningen 1897 och 1800-talets världsutställningar* (Stockholm: Nordiska museets förlag, 1994).

Ekström, Anders, Solveig Jülich & Pelle Snickars (eds), *1897: Mediehistorier kring Stockholmsutställningen* (Stockholm: SLBA, 2006).

Ekström, Anders, Solveig Jülich & Pelle Snickars (eds), "Inledning: I mediearkivet", in Ekström, Jülich & Snickars, (eds), *1897: Mediehistorier kring Stockholmsutställningen* (Stockholm: SLBA, 2006).

Ellenius, Allan, *Den offentliga konsten och ideologierna: Studier över verk från 1800- och 1900-talen* (Stockholm: Almqvist & Wicksell, 1971).

Florin, Bo, *Den nationella stilen: Studier i den svenska filmens guldålder* (Stockholm: Aura förlag, 1997).

Fritz, Birgitta, "Kung Magnus Erikssons planer för Vadstena klosterkyrka – och Birgittas", in Steinar Supphellen (ed), *Kongsmenn og krossmenn: Festskrift til Grethe Authén Blom* (Trondheim: Tapir forlag, 1992).

Fritz, Birgitta, "Vadstena klosterkyrka och kung Magnus testamente 1346", in Per Beskow & Annette Landen (eds), *Birgitta av Vadstena: Pilgrim och profet 1303-1373: En jubileumsbok* (Stockholm: Natur & Kultur, 2003).

Fröjmark, Anders, *Mirakler och helgonkult: Linköpings biskopsdöme under senmedeltiden* (Uppsala: Uppsala University, 1992).

Furhammar, Leif, *Filmen i Sverige: En historia i tio kapitel och en fortsättning* (1991; Stockholm: Dialogos/Svenska filminstitutet, 2003).

Gejrot, Claes (ed), *Vadstenadiariet: Latinsk text med översättning och kommentar* (Stockholm: Samfundet för utgivande av handskrifter rörande Skandinaviens historia, 1996).

Green, Abigail, *Fatherlands: Statue-Building and Nationhood in Nineteenth Century Germany* (Cambridge: Cambridge University Press, 2001).

Grundberg, Malin, *Ceremoniernas makt: Maktöverföring och genus i Vasatidens kungliga ceremonier* (Lund: Nordic Academic Press, 2005).

Gustafsson [Reinius], Lotten, "Bocken brinner! En dialog på offentlig plats och i Gävles lokalpress", in Barbro Klein (ed), *Gatan är vår! Ritualer på offentliga platser* (Stockholm: Carlssons, 1995).

Gustafsson, Tommy, "Filmen som historisk källa: Historiografi, pluralism och representativitet", *Historisk tidskrift* 2006 (3).

Gustafsson, Tommy, *En fiende till civilisationen: Manlighet, genusrelationer, sexualitet och rasstereotyper i svensk filmkultur under 1920-talet* (Lund: Sekel bokförlag, 2007).

Habermas, Jürgen, *The Structural Transformation of the Public Sphere* (1962; Cambridge: Polity Press, 1989).

Hall, Stuart, "The Determination of News Photographs", in Stanley Cohen & Jock Young (eds), *The Manufacture of News: Social Problems, Deviance and the Mass Media* (London: Constable, 1973).

Hartley, John, *Popular Reality: Journalism, Modernity, Popular Culture* (London: Arnold, 1996).

Hirdman, Yvonne, *Att lägga livet tillrätta: Studier i svensk folkhemspolitik* (Stockholm: Carlssons, 1989).

Hobsbawm, Eric, & Terence Ranger (eds), *The Invention of Tradition* (Cambridge: Cambridge University Press, 1983).

Holmberg, Åke, *Skandinavismen i Sverige: Vid 1800-talets mitt (1843-1863)* (Göteborg, 1946).

Holmberg, Sören, & Lennart Weibull (eds), *Skilda världar: Trettiåtta kapitel om politik, medier och samhälle* (Göteborg: SOM-institutet, 2008).

Homans, Margaret, & Adrienne Munich (eds), *Remaking Queen Victoria* (Cambridge: Cambridge University Press, 1997).

Hunt, Lynn, *Politics, Culture, and Class in the French Revolution* (Berkeley: University of California Press, 1986).

Iggers, George G., *Historiography in the Twentieth Century: From Scientific Objectivity to the Postmodern Challenge* (Hanover: Wesleyan University Press, 1997).

Jansson, Maria, Maria Wendt & Cecilia Åse, "Kön och nation i vardag och vetenskap", *Statsvetenskaplig tidskrift* 2007 (3).

Jansson, Sven-Bertil (ed), *Engelbrektskrönikan* (Stockholm: Tiden, 1994).

Järbe, Bengt, *Stockholms statyer* (Stockholm: Byggförl./Kultur, 1997).

Johannesson, Eric, "August Blanche, den ädle folkvännen", in Kurt Johannisson *et al.*, *Heroer på offentlighetens scen: Politiker och publicister i Sverige 1809-1914* (Stockholm: Tiden, 1987).

Jönsson, Mats, *Film och historia: Historisk hollywoodfilm 1960-2000* (Lund: KFS, 2004).

Jönsson, Mats, "'Den kungliga skölden': Per Albin Hansson, Gustaf V och medierna", in Mats Jönsson & Pelle Snickars (eds), *Medier och politik: Om arbetarrörelsens mediestrategier under 1900-talet* (Stockholm: SLBA, 2007).

Jönsson, Mats, & Pelle Snickars (eds), *Medier & politik: Om arbetarrörelsens mediestrategier under 1900-talet* (Stockholm: SLBA, 2007).

Keen, Andrew, *The Cult of the Amateur: How Today's Internet Is Killing Our Culture* (New York: Doubleday, 2007).

Kjellén, Alf, *Sociala idéer och motiv hos svenska författare under 1830- och 1840-talen*, II, *(1844-1848): Från patriarkalism till marxism* (Stockholm, 1950).

Knopp, Guido, *Majestät! Die letzten großen Monarchien* (München: Bertelsmann, 2006).

Koivunen, Anu, "Moderns kropp, fädrens land: Nationell film som könsteknologi", in Tytti Soila (ed), *Dialoger: Feministisk filmteori i praktik* (Stockholm: Aura, 1997).

Krigström, Erik, *Swartz – en släkt i Norrköping: Stadshistorisk utställning 1959-1960* (Norrköping: Norrköpings museum, 1959).

Landes, Joan B., *Visualizing the Nation: Gender, Representation and Revolution in Eighteenth-Century France* (Ithaca & London: Cornell University Press, 2001).

Lewis, Katherine J., "Becoming a Virgin King: Richard II and Edward the Confessor", in Samantha J.E. Riches & Sarah Salih (eds), *Gender and Holiness: Men, Women and Saints in Late Medieval Europe* (London: Routledge 2002).

Linderborg, Åsa, *Socialdemokraterna skriver historia: Historieskrivning som ideologisk maktresurs, 1892-2000* (Stockholm: Atlas, 2001).

Lindgren, Mereth, "De heliga änkorna: S. Anna-kultens framväxt, speglad i birgittinsk ikonografi", *Konsthistorisk tidskrift* 1990 (1-2).

Löfgren, Orvar, "Nationella arenor", in Billy Ehn *et al.* (eds), *Försvenskningen av Sverige: Det nationellas förvandlingar* (Stockholm: Natur & Kultur, 1993).

Lundell, Patrik, "Pressen är budskapet: Journalistkongressen och den svenska pressens legitimitetssträvanden", in Anders Ekström, Solveig Jülich & Pelle Snickars (eds), *1897: Mediehistorier kring Stockholmsutställningen* (Stockholm: SLBA, 2006).

Lundell, Patrik, "The Medium is the Message: The Media History of the Press", *Media History* 2008 (1).

Maffesoli, Michael, *The Time of the Tribes* (London: Sage, 1996).

Manguel, Alberto, *A History of Reading* (London: Flamingo, 1997).

McClintock, Anne, *Imperial Leather: Race, Gender and Sexuality in the Imperial Contest* (New York & London: Routledge, 1995).

Miller, Daniel, "Materiality: An Introduction", in Daniel Miller (ed), *Materiality* (Durham, N.C.: Duke University Press, 2005).

Miscovici, Serge, *Social Representation: Exploration in Social Psychology* (Cambridge: Polity Press, 2000).

Moland, Tallak, "Konstruksjon av mandighet i det nordlige landskapet: Om Fridtjof Nansens polarferder ved århundreskiftet", in Anne Marie Berggren (ed), *Manligt och omanligt i ett historiskt perspektiv* (Stockholm: Forskningsrådsnämnden, 1999).

Mosse, George L., *Fallen Soldiers: Reshaping the Memory of the World Wars* (New York: Oxford University Press, 1990).

Mostov, Julie, "Sexing the Nation/Desexing the Body: Politics of National Identity in Former Yugoslavia", in Tamar Mayer (ed), *Gender Ironies of Nationalism: Sexing the Nation* (London & New York: Routledge, 2000).

Mumford, Lewis, *The Culture of Cities* (New York: Hartcourt, Brace and Company, 1938).

Nye, Joseph, *Soft Power* (New York: PublicAffairs, 2004).

Oredsson, Sverker, *Svensk rädsla: Offentlig fruktan i Sverige under 1900-talets första hälft* (Lund: Nordic Academic Press, 2001).

O'Reilly, Tom, "Web 2.0 Compact Definition: Trying Again" – http://radar.oreilly.com/2006/12/web-20-compact-definition-tryi.html (15 August 2008).

Overud, Johanna, *I beredskap med Fru Lojal: Behovet av kvinnlig arbetskraft i Sverige under andra världskriget* (Stockholm: Almqvist & Wiksell, 2005).

Phillips, Louise, "Media Discourse and the Danish Monarchy: Reconciling Egalitarianism and Royalism", *Media, Culture & Society* 1999 (2).

Plunkett, John, *Queen Victoria: First Media Monarch* (Oxford: Oxford University Press, 2003).

Popova, Susanna, *Överklass: En bok om klass och identitet* (Stockholm: Lind & Co., 2007).

Qvist, Per Olov, *Folkhemmets bilder: Modernisering, motstånd och mentalitet i den svenska 30-talsfilmen* (Lund: Arkiv förlag, 1995).

Resic, Sanimir, *American Warriors in Vietnam: Warrior Values and the Myth of the War Experience During the Vietnam War, 1965-1973* (Lund: Lund University, 1999).

Riches, Samantha J.E., "St George as a Male Virgin Martyr", in Samantha J.E. Riches & Sarah Salih (eds), *Gender and Holiness: Men, Women and Saints in Late Medieval Europe* (London: Routledge 2002).

Rodell, Magnus, "Att gjuta en nation: Om statyinvigningar i Sverige på 1800-talet", unpublished MA-thesis, Department of History of Science and Ideas (Uppsala, 1996).

Rodell, Magnus, *Att gjuta en nation: Statyinvigningar och nationsformering i Sverige vid 1800-talets mitt* (Stockholm: Natur & Kultur, 2002).

Rodell, Magnus, "Teknikens heroer: Pansarskepp och ångturbiner som ett svenskt kulturarv", in Peter Aronsson & Magdalena Hillström (eds), *Kulturarvets dynamik: Det institutionaliserade kulturarvets förändringar* (Linköping: Linköping University, 2005).

Rodell, Magnus, "Fallna soldater och fortifikationer i vildmarken: Det ryska hotet och medielandskapet kring 1900", in Leif Dahlberg & Pelle Snickars (eds), *Berättande i olika medier* (Stockholm: SLBA, 2008).

Schudson, Michael, *Discovering the News: A Social History of American Newspapers* (New York: Basic Books, 1978).

Shapiro, Michael J., "The Politics of the 'Family'", in Judy Dean (ed), *Cultural Studies and Political Theory* (Ithaca & London: Cornell University Press, 2000).

Shirky, Clay, *Here Comes Everybody: The Power of Organizing without Organizations* (New York: Penguin Press, 2008).

Smith, Dorothy E., *Texts, Facts and Femininity: Exploring the Relations of Ruling* (London: Routledge, 1990).

Smith, Jeffrey R., "The Monarchy versus the Nation: The 'Festive Year' 1913 in Wilhelmine Germany", *German Studies Review* 2002 (2).

Snickars, Pelle, "Bildrutor i minnets film: Om medieprins Wilhelm och film som käll- och åskåd-ningsmaterial", in Pelle Snickars & Cecilia Trenter (eds), *Det förflutna som film och vice versa: Om medierade historiebruk* (Lund: Studentlitteratur, 2004).

Snickars, Pelle, "Prins Wilhelm och politikens medialisering" *Ord & Bild* 2006 (1).

Söderlind, Solfrid, *Porträttbruk i Sverige 1840-1865: En funktions- och interaktionsstudie* (Stockholm: Carlssons, 1993).

Söderlind, Solfrid, "Den leuchtenbergska kopplingen", *Artes: Tidskrift för litteratur, konst och musik* 1997 (4).

Sontag, Susan, "Women", in Annie Leibovitz & Susan Sontag, *Women* (New York: Random House, 1999).

Sörensen, Thomas, *Det blänkande eländet: En bok om kronprinsens husarer i sekelskiftets Malmö* (Lund: Lund University, 1997).

Strohm, Paul, *England's Empty Throne: Usurpation and the Language of Legitimation, 1399–1422* (New Haven & London: Yale University Press, 1998).

Tegenborg Falkdalen, Karin, *Kungen är en kvinna: Retorik och praktik kring kvinnliga monarker under tidigmodern tid* (Umeå: Department of Historical Studies, 2003).

Thompson, John B., *The Media and Modernity: A Social Theory of the Media* (Cambridge: Polity Press, 1999).

Tjeder, David, "Konsten att blifva herre öfver hvarje lidelse: Den ständigt hotade manligheten", in Anne Marie Berggren (ed), *Manligt och omanligt i ett historiskt perspektiv* (Stockholm: Forskningsrådsnämnden, 1999).

Toplin, Robert Brent, *Reel History: In Defense of Hollywood* (Lawrence: University Press of Kansas, 2002).

Tornbjer, Charlotte, *Den nationella modern: Moderskap i konstruktioner av nationell svensk gemenskap under 1900-talets första hälft.* (Lund: Department of History, 2002).

Towns, Ann, "Paradoxes of (In)Equality: Something is Rotten in the Gender Equal State of Sweden", *Cooperation and Conflict* 2002 (2).

Wahlström, Bengt, *Guide till det virtuella samhället* (Stockholm: SNS Förlag, 2007).

Walzer, Michael, "On the Role of Symbolism in Political Thought", *Political Science Quarterly* 1967 (82).

Wichman, Knut, *Från Karl Johanstidens Norrköping* (Göteborg: Föreningen Gamla Norrköping, 1957).

Windt, Franziska, et al. (eds), *Die Kaiser und die Macht der Medien* (Berlin: Jaron Verlag, 2005).

Young, James E., *The Texture of Memory: Holocaust Memorials and Meaning* (New Haven & London: Yale University Press, 1993).

Yuval-Davis, Nira, *Gender and Nation* (London: Sage, 1997).

Zander, Ulf, *Fornstora dagar, moderna tider: Bruket av och debatter om svensk historia från sekelskifte till sekelskifte* (Lund: Nordic Academic Press, 2001).

Žižek, Slavoj, *The Sublime Object of Ideology* (London: Verso, 1989).

Contributors

Cecilia Åse, PhD, is Lecturer at the Department of Political Science, Stockholm University. Her dissertation *Makten att se* was published in 2000, and analyses women's subordination, in particular how the modus operandi of subordination rests on women's embodiment. Åse's main research interest has thereafter been the relationship between gender and nation. She has published articles on feminist and political theory, and is presently working on a research project on monarchy and democracy in Sweden 1970 to 2000.

Louise Berglund, PhD, is Senior Lecturer in History at Örebro University. Her main area of research is political culture and gender relations in the Late Middle Ages. In her dissertation, *Guds stat och maktens villkor* (2003), she analyses sermons as sources of political thought and ambitions. In the area of visual culture and gender, Berglund has worked within a multidisciplinary research programme. In her current field of research, she studies the political communication of queens during the Middle Ages, particularly Queen Philippa.

Mattias Frihammar is PhD-student and teaches Ethnology at Stockholm University. His dissertation focuses contemporary royalty in Sweden and studies the ways in which royal exclusivity, authenticity and authority are created, maintained, and sometimes challenged. In 2005, Frihammar published "Idrott och kunglighet: Victoriadagen på Öland" in the anthology *Tankar från baslinjen: Humanister om idrott, kropp och hälsa*.

Tommy Gustafsson has a PhD in History and is Lecturer in Film Studies at Lund University. In 2008, he published his dissertation, *En fiende till civilisationen*, on masculinity, gender relations, sexuality, and racial stereotyping in Swedish film culture in the 1920s. He has also published articles in *Cinema Journal* (on Oscar Micheaux) and *Film International* (on transnational biopics).

Mats Jönsson, PhD, is a Research Fellow in Film Studies at Lund University and Senior Lecturer in Film Studies at Örebro University. His dissertation was published in 2004 and analyses historical Hollywood film as source material. He has co-authored one monograph and co-edited two interdisciplinary anthologies about Swedish documentaries. His recent publications mainly focus historical, archival and documentary issues. Two of his ongoing projects deal with Nazi newsreels in Sweden and films about the city of Lund.

Patrik Lundell, PhD, is a Research Fellow at the Department of Culture Studies, Linköping University. Lundell's dissertation, *Pressen i provinsen*, on changes in editorial ideals ca. 1750 to 1850, was published in 2002. His latest book, the co-edited anthology *Mediernas kulturhistoria* (2008), concerns the cultural history of the media. Lundell has also published several articles on the media history of the press, for example in *Media History*.

Magnus Rodell, PhD, is Lecturer in History of Science and Ideas at Uppsala University. His dissertation, *Att gjuta en nation*, a study of statues and nation-building in nineteenth century Sweden, was published in 2002. Rodell has published several articles on monuments, memory and place, for example in the anthologies *Memory Work* (2005) and *Grenzregionen* (2007). He is currently working on a project on the making and commemoration of borders.

Pelle Snickars, PhD, is Head of Research at the National Library of Sweden. He is co-editor of a number of books; among them two recent anthologies on narration in the media and on the cultural history of the media, *Berättande i olika medier* and *Mediernas kulturhistoria*, respectively. Currently, Snickars is preparing a volume on the video sharing site YouTube, *The YouTube Reader*, to be published in 2009.

Kristina Widestedt, PhD, is Senior Lecturer in journalism and media studies at the Department of Journalism, Media and Communication, Stockholm University. Her dissertation, *Ett tongivande förnuft*, was published in 2001 and studies two centuries of music criticism in Swedish dailies.

Index